OUTRAGEOUS
FORTUNE

Disclaimer

The views and information contained in this book are those of the West family and their associates and do not necessarily reflect the views of the publishers. *The West Family Album* in no way endorses consumption of illicit drugs, excessive drinking, promiscuity, foul language or safe-cracking.

OUTRAGEOUS FORTUNE

The West Family Album

Rachel Lang, James Griffin and Tim Balme

Published by Libro International, an imprint of Oratia Media Ltd, 783 West Coast Road, Oratia, Auckland 0604, New Zealand (www.oratiamedia.com); and South Pacific Pictures Ltd, 8 Tolich Place, Auckland 0654, New Zealand (www.southpacificpictures.com)

Copyright © 2009 Oratia Media & South Pacific Pictures
Photographs © 2005–2009 South Pacific Pictures Ltd
Photography by Jae Frew, Caren Hastings and Steve King
'The 7 deadly sins of Van and Jethro West' kindly reproduced courtesy of *New Idea*

The authors assert their moral rights in the work.

This book is protected by copyright. Except for the purposes of fair reviewing, no part of this publication may be reproduced or transmitted in any form or by any means, whether electronic, digital or mechanical, including photocopying, recording, any digital or computerised format, or any information storage and retrieval system, including by any means via the Internet, without permission in writing from the publisher. Infringers of copyright render themselves liable to prosecution.

All characters appearing in this work are fictitious. Any resemblance to real persons, living or dead, is purely coincidental.

ISBN 978-1-877514-00-5
First published 2009

Project managers: Carolyn Lagahetau and Tamar Münch
Writers: Rachel Lang, James Griffin and Tim Balme
Designer: Cheryl Rowe, Macarn Design
Photo research: Lucy Ewen, Heather Jensen

Outrageous Fortune is broadcast in New Zealand on TV3 with funding from NZ On Air.

Printed in China by Nordica

Contents

Introduction – Vern Gardiner (MNZOM) 8
The West family tree with roots 10
'From now on, we play it straight.' 12
Recipes from the West 13
Cheryl West on childcare 16
Pascalle's words of beauty and wisdom 18
You can tell a lot about a girl from what's in her handbag... 20
Loretta's blog – defining moments 22
School reports 26
Wolfgang West: an interview 30
The 7 deadly sins of Van and Jethro West 32
Ted West's guide to gambling 34
The Tool Guy Code 36
Munter's guide to a gud time 38
Wayne Judd 41
Tips on living with the Wests 42
A neighbour speaks 44
Department of Social Welfare report: Nicky and Sheree Greegan 46

Letter to the editor   47
West associates: where are they now?   48
The official Outrageous Fortune trivia quiz   51
The official Outrageous Fortune drinking game   54
Acting up – interviews with the cast   57
Behind the scenes...   66
Episode summaries   68
Quiz answers   79

Introduction — Vern Gardiner (MNZOM)
West Auckland City Councillor (Greater Titirangi Ward)

West Auckland City Council
We taiao o West Auckland

When the publishers approached me to say they were doing a book on the West family, I admit I thought they were, to use the vernacular, 'taking the piss'. Even when they explained that the Wests represent a very real part of West Auckland society I was still at pains to understand why this particular sub-section of the cultural melting-pot that is West Auckland needed to be immortalised in print. At the end of the day, I guess, a celebration of diversity, by definition, celebrates even the most divergent elements.

I have known the Wests and their extended family of 'associates' for many years. When I first arrived in New Zealand, from Wales, with my parents, at age 14, we moved into a house on Aztec Road. Our neighbours were Theodore 'Ted' West and his wife, Rita.

Rita was the most engaging of our new neighbours, while to us immigrants, fresh off the boat, Ted was a mysterious figure who seemed to enjoy mimicking our accents and suggesting over the fence that Wales was, perhaps, where we should return to. Was his habit of urinating on the lawn, we wondered, a New Zealand-wide custom or just him?

It was only later, after visits from the police seeking information as to Ted's whereabouts, that we became aware of Ted's reputation as one of New Zealand's foremost safecrackers. Knowing that, many of the goings-on in that house on Aztec Road suddenly made sense — the groups of men who would assemble there then drive off into the night; Rita's nocturnal sessions burying things in the garden; the long, long periods Rita would be alone in the house … I remember clearly Ted's reply the day my father broached the subject of his career with him. 'Don't you worry, ya leek muncher,' he said over the fence. 'Everyone knows you don't piss in your own nest.' I found this quite odd given that he was urinating against the fence at the time.

It was Rita West who opened up to me and through her I was introduced to a whole new range of experiences that were far removed from my childhood in Wales. In many ways it was she who turned me into the man I am today — and in at least one of the West children I see many of the same qualities Rita West possessed.

So what are the qualities that define a West and make them worthy of a whole book? Like many people who dwell in West Auckland, they have a certain singularity of purpose in everything they do. Ruthless is a word that springs to mind. They certainly don't let trifling matters like the law get between them and what they seek. There are some, I suppose, who might see that as an admirable trait.

There is also, if one thinks hard enough, an admirable vibrancy about the West clan. Their love of life and their ability to grab said life by the balls, if necessary, is something many West Aucklanders can relate to — even if the Wests do tend to squeeze a tad hard once they have the balls of life in their grasp.

And so it is my pleasure, both as West Auckland Councillor for the Greater Titirangi Ward and someone who has known the West family, to declare this book well and truly open. I look forward to reading it myself (possibly in the presence of my lawyer) and I hope that everyone who does read it will take what they find in the spirit in which it is intended.

Best of luck,

Vern Gardiner

The West family tree with roots

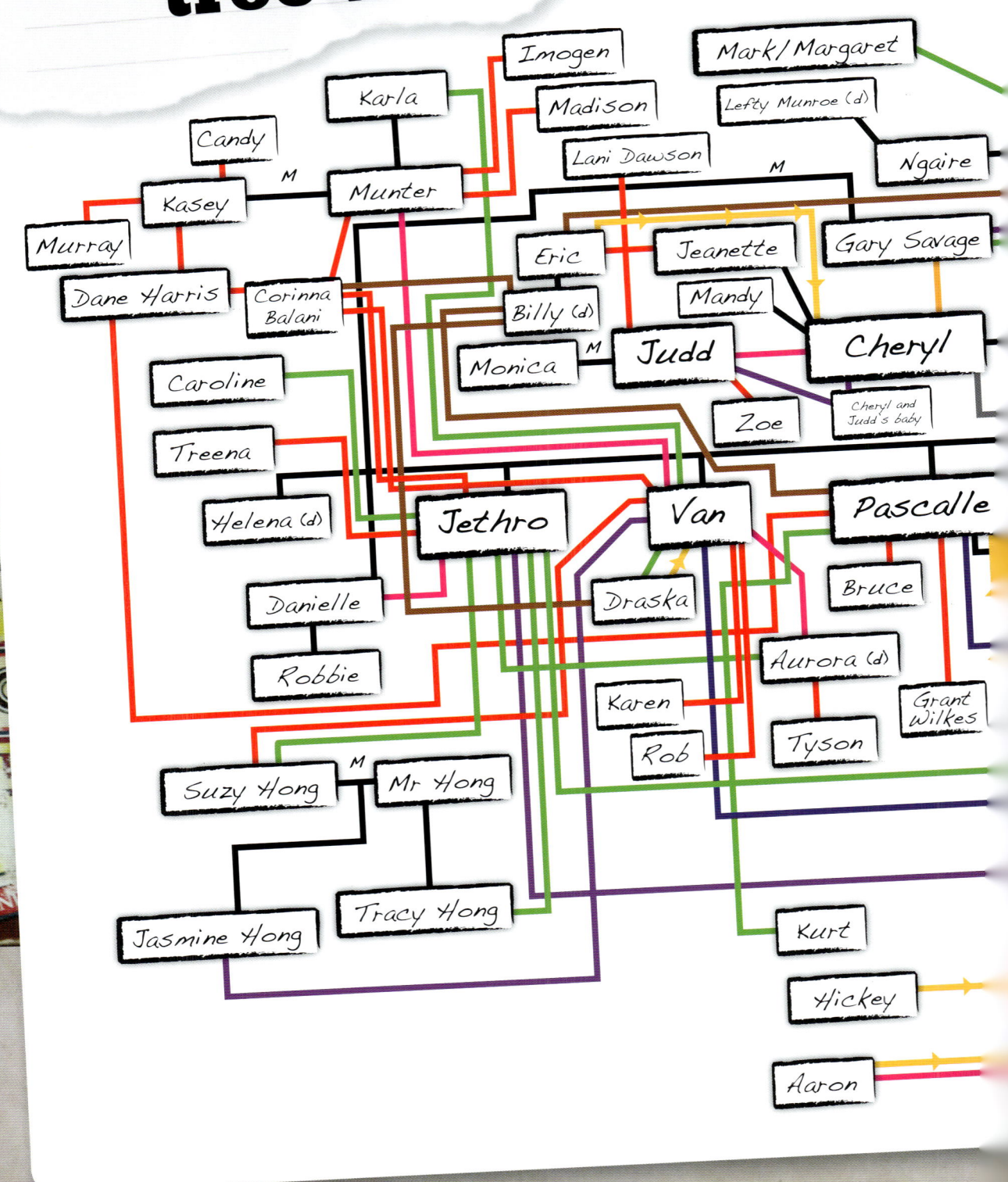

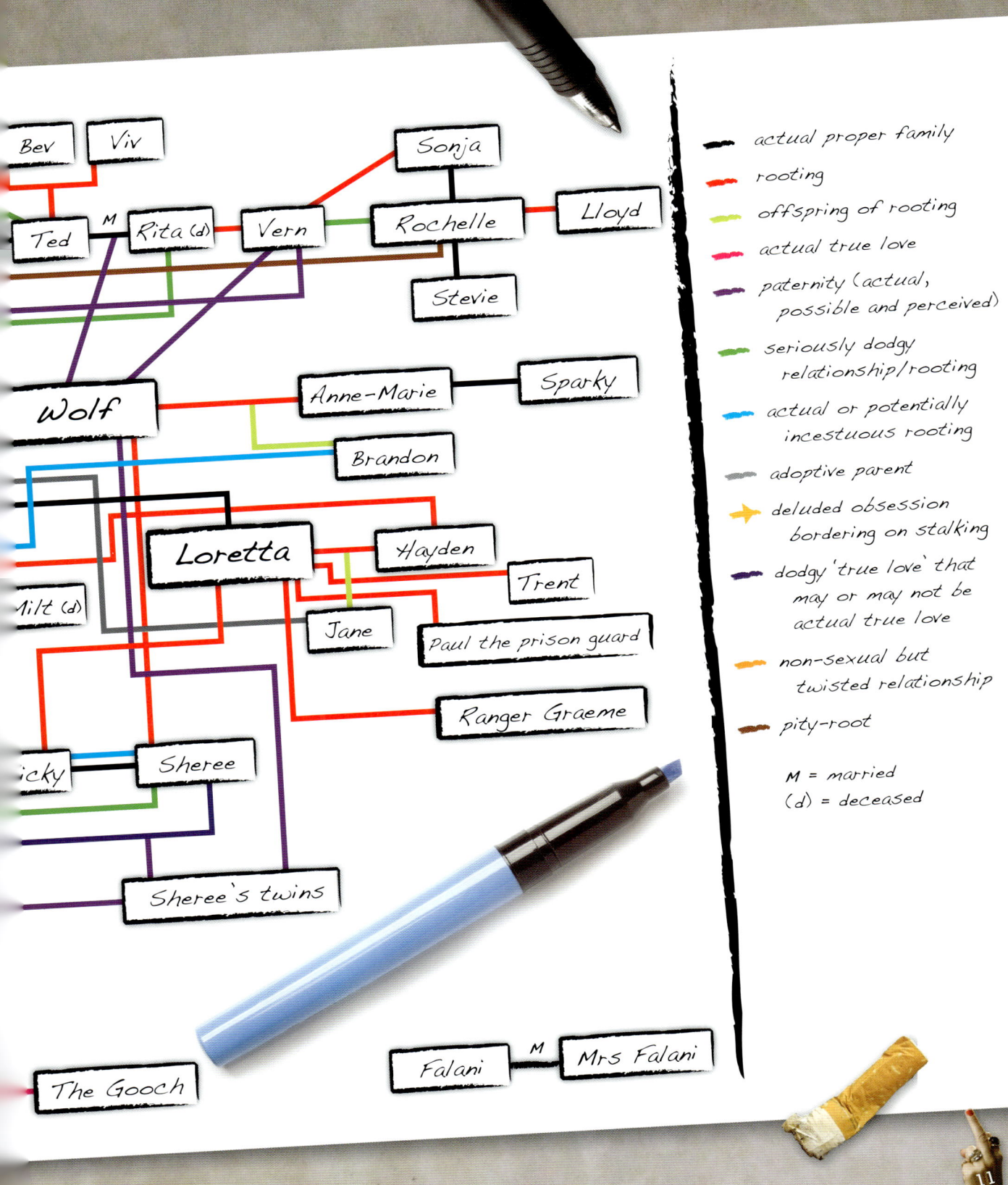

The West family tree with roots

'From now on, we play it straight.'

Cheryl West
Series 1, episode 1 *Slings and Arrows*

Outrageous Fortune, Episode 1, Published Script

45   INT. WEST HOUSE (LIVING AREA) - DAY   45

      CHERYL
You start work for them tomorrow — which is a bloody sight better than prison, wouldn't you agree? Your dad went into prison today for four years. He's going to miss out on the next four years of your lives — and we're treating it like ... like it's an occupational hazard! Well, not any more. It all stops. Right here. Right now. From now on, we play it straight.

      VAN
What do you mean, "straight"?

      CHERYL
I mean we are out of the crime business. We are not bludging off welfare any more. And we are getting a fucking education. And I ... I'm out of the shop. No more dirty money, I'm gonna get myself a real job. And today ... today we're gonna celebrate the example your brother has set us, that just because we're Wests doesn't mean we have to be criminals. Right. Good. I'll do my hair and then we'll go.

Well, you know my motto, Cheryl? Where there's a crime, there's a member of the West family.
      Judd

CONFIDENTIAL

Recipes from the West

I got asked to put in some recipes for this book, which is a bit weird because it's not like I'm Alison Holst or anything and actually Wayne (that's Wayne Judd) is a much better cook than me. He does marinating and stuff with garlic and spices. So anyway I thought I'd just put in some bits of my recipe book. It's not really a recipe book, it's actually one of Van's old exercise books from Chris Amon Primary but since he never wrote in it and it was lying around I started sticking recipes in it and he never missed it.

Rochelle's Party Dip – Makes Heaps!

8 packs onion soup mix
8 tins reduced cream
8 caps vinegar

Mix

This one's really good for parties and I always keep a lot of packets of soup mix in the cupboard because I always think bugger it and buy ten of everything, because you never know when you're going to run out. BUT be careful about putting this in too big a bowl because things can easily get lost like people's car keys and ciggie butts and then you only find them at the end of the party which is sometimes not until the next morning.

Fish Pie

Quite a few spuds, about three or four cups-full when you've boiled and mashed them
salt and pepper
milk and butter
25 g butter
1 tbsp flour
1 cup milk
500 g tin of smoked fish
2 chopped hardboiled eggs

Boil your potatoes and mash them with the milk and a bit of butter and bung in some salt and pepper to taste. Then make a white sauce with the butter, flour and milk. Put in the smoked fish and hardboiled eggs and some chopped parsley if you want to. Sometimes I put in a bit of onion soup mix for flavouring. I never do.

Put the fish mix in a baking dish, top with potatoes and maybe a bit of butter, then bung in the oven at 180°C until pale golden. If you want you can put sliced tomatoes on the top but that's usually only for special occasions.

Makes enough for 4 to 6, but otherwise you can double the amount and stick it in a bigger dish.

I've been making fish pie since forever, and my mum used to make it too. This was because my parents had a dairy and Mum needed to use up tins of fish that had been sitting round too long. Stock rotation is the fancy name for this. Actually my Mum's cooking was pretty much always things you could find in our dairy on stock rotation because she always said there didn't seem much bloody point in running a shop and still having to go to the bloody supermarket. She said 'bloody' a lot my mother, which is why I usually think of my big sister as Bloody Jeanette and my little sister as Bloody Mandy. But sometimes Mum didn't mean it unkindly.

Anyway I've been making fish pie for years and no one gave me any gyp about it until lately — they just ate it. And if they didn't eat it would be bread and jam or go down the bloody takeaway then. Wayne seems to think fish pie is better with smoked kawai (I'm not sure how you spell that). But this seems a bit fancy to me or perhaps it's a Maori thing but at the rate my lot eat, Van or Ted would be bound to choke on a bone so I don't think it's safe. That's never a worry if you use smoked fish from a tin. There's been quite a bit of talk about Pascalle's fish pie but my suspicion is she didn't make it at all, she just bought it. Pascalle brought a lasagne round the other day and she said she made it herself, but it still had the price tag underneath so you can see why I'm suspicious. *I did so make it.*

So anyway, there's my recipe.

I did so make it. Mum is just jealous.

Kasey's Eggplant Thing

I'm putting in Kasey's eggplant thing because she was pestering me about it and saying she was sure there would be lots of requests for it and there would also be some very upset people if it wasn't included, like her and Munter.

I haven't actually made this myself because from what I can see, eggplants are like a sponge in vegetable form and what they are mostly good at is soaking up oil. But if you like eggplants then maybe you will like this.

But we do all really love Kasey's eggplant thing and I'm not only just saying that because she might read this book and would be offended if I said anything bad about the eggplant thing. And I'm not saying anything bad about it except that eggplants are not everyone's favourite food and possibly not as popular as roast pork.

Hey Cher!! You said you loved this when you and Wayne came round here so here is the recipe!! It's really easy and I made it up myself. ☺

My Eggplant Thing

3 eggplants cut into slices
oil, lots for frying
garlic, 5 cloves, chopped
pasta sauce — any kind will do
some basil leaves
curry powder
mozzarella or other cheese

Fry the eggplant in the oil until it's squashy. Then fry the garlic in oil and add it to the eggplant with some curry powder — maybe a tablespoon? Get creative!
Layer the spiced eggplant and pasta sauce with basil leaves and bake with the mozzarella on top.
It's a bit Indian with a bit of Italian and it's Yum!!

Recipes from the West

Cheryl West on childcare

I often get asked about kids and how to raise them. I say that I am no bloody expert, and I never read a book on any of it and I fell out with Plunket when they said that Van was a bit sub. I'm sure they meant well but still they didn't have to say it.

But anyway, here's what I think and you can take it or leave it. Because kids are mostly as you find them and never what you think they will be and they are always a big surprise. Mine are anyway.

Love

The important thing with kids is that you love them to bits, even when they're being right little shits. But this definitely doesn't mean you have to lie on the floor and let them walk all over you or give in to them just because they're throwing a wobbly over lollies at the supermarket. I see this all the time down at the supermarket and it makes me wild. But I don't like seeing people smacking kids all the time either and I sometimes see this at the supermarket and it makes me even wilder. So I generally ask those people if they want a smack themselves and that often sorts them out. Or maybe they just need a break because it's bloody hard dealing with toddlers who are like Ted but more so.

Food

Kids should eat what's on the table (though preferably it should be food. You might think I'm joking here but Van ate a place mat once. He was a bit out of it at the time). A lot of kids nowadays are really fussy and their mums run round after them, making them fancy things and cutting up fruit so it looks like origami. I say bugger that for a game of soldiers. The fact is if you're a mother you've got your work cut out for you already and in my experience kids won't starve and if they're hungry they'll eat it eventually. (Unless they're Loretta but she's not a normal child.)

What you do is stick the food on the table and if they don't like it they can make something themselves or have bread and jam or go down the bloody takeaway. This is a bit hard to enforce when they're younger but actually Van and Jethro have been nipping off to the Golden Dragon since they were about six.

Freedom

These days kids aren't allowed out on their own on account of traffic and weirdos, and this is a shame. My kids have always been good round traffic, possibly because of all the cars haring up and down our driveway and also going to stock cars. My kids had also met people like Eric, Sparky and Falani so they were used to weirdos. Kids should be allowed out on their own, even if it's just nipping off down the Golden Dragon or going over to John Rowles Park to let off firecrackers in the rubbish tins.

Interests
Kids should be encouraged to follow their interests, especially ones that aren't too dangerous or involve driving under the age of 12. Though if that's what they're into it can be hard to stop them. If they want to do ballet or Irish dancing or any of that stuff then personally I think it's a good thing. But my rule is if they start a thing they have to finish it and usually they should get themselves there too. All this being a taxi service is ruining our kids and it's not much fun for mothers either.

Drugs and drink
They're both bad for you but you're not going to stop them. So the best thing to do is not make a song and dance about it because if you've got kids like mine that only encourages them, especially when they're teenagers. And it's also hard to have a rum and coke yourself if you're saying they can't. But when they do come home rat-faced you've got choices: let them suffer and have the hangover from hell, or get them to hurl. Salty water is my usual way. That's not nice either.

Bad shit happening to kids
When I read in the paper about the terrible things people are doing to their kids and leaving them with crap people, it makes me wild. Perhaps you might be worried about Jane because she does get passed around a bit. But I don't leave her with anyone I don't trust and she's looking pretty good on it and Plunket say she's advanced. (Though I'm hoping she's not as advanced as Loretta or she will be dangerous.) And she does swimming and going to play group and things we never had in my day. I suppose they're good but my kids just used to do stuff out the back and annoy the neighbours which Jethro says was very educational. And he's got a degree so it can't have been all bad.

But anyway kids are the most precious bloody thing in the world. And if you think bad shit is happening to some kid you know then you should call someone or ask for help because that's not dobbing in my book.
    Or if you called me, then I would sort them out.
    But the main thing is love your kids and be honest. I don't always say what I think but I don't hold back either.

Cheryl West on childcare

Pascalle's words of beauty and wisdom

As taped by Alistair Purvis (formerly of the Janet Frame Rest Home; now a resident at the Maud Basham Sunshine Villas in Merivale, Christchurch), shortly after Pascalle's break-up with Bruce.

Pascalle on gratitude

Every day I get up out of bed and think how lucky I am to be able to get up, and that I have a bed, though I'm not sharing it with anyone right now.

That's not a come-on, okay! Even though my engagement to a doctor ended recently.

And I'm not going to say his name, except it starts with B and he's from Pukekohe, but now he's in Wellington, which my sister says is punishment enough. I don't hate people from Wellington (though God knows why they live there) and I'm also not hoping that a Force 10 gale will hurl Bruce down Lambton Quay into an oncoming truck or anything like that.

Because my work with the elderly has made me realise everyone suffers, almost as much as me.

So I've got heaps of reasons to be grateful. Heaps.

Pascalle on beauty

'Everyone is beautiful, in their own way.'

I don't know who said that, but it was someone very wise, or from the Bible. I can see beauty in everyone I work with, and I think they see it in me too.

Not just because I'm attractive and have a good skincare routine, but because I've got inner beauty.

Which is mostly what the elderly have, obviously, given that they're like, old.

Pascalle on the wonders of nature

Nature inspires me. I love nature: the trees, the bushes, the grassy things that are probably grass. Everyone is full of nature, and trees remind me of old people because they bend with the wind, and creak a bit sometimes. But they're really rooted as well.

Not as in totally poked; as in, they have grace, but they're not too fast on their feet. And trees don't have feet — everyone knows that — they have roots.

I guess that's the main thing here, we all need to be more like trees — have roots and be rooted.

For full copies of the Purvis Tapes, write c/o Tool Enterprises, PO Box 104-124, Lincoln North, Auckland 0654. Enclose a cheque for $150 (incl. p+p) made out to L. West.

West Auckland Chronicle

Internet: www.wachronicle.co.nz Friday, March 27th 2009 MY PLACE - MY PAPER?

ANNUAL COMMUNITY AWARDS
SOCIAL HEROES AWARD 2008 FOR COMMUNITY ENGAGEMENT
The Voting Papers are on Page 6

West Auckland's Most Stylish Bag Lady

By Chris Colano

"I believe in West Auckland," says the young businesswoman. "It's a place where anything is possible, no matter what their background."

Pascalle West describes her new bag, The Best Bag Ever as the "only bag you will ever need".

The young West Aucklander's new product is made in Henderson Valley and is selling throughout the country.

The young businesswoman is only 22, and grew up in West Auckland. She's also a recent widow, who has taken strength from her new invention. She believes that it will change the lives of women, as it has changed hers.

Ms West says her bag is the culmination of many careers, first as a successful model, then as a caregiver at a local rest home, where she taught exercise classes. She then had an international career as an inspirational and motivational speaker and exercise guru, though a planned TV series did not eventuate.

"My husband had just died, and I didn't feel it was appropriate for me to continue with the project," says Ms West, whose voice breaks a little as she speaks of her American husband, millionaire Milton Delaney III.

"What was so great about Milt was that he saw the positive in everyone, even my family, who were not very welcoming to him."

She believes their attitude may have contributed to the heart attack which claimed his life.

"While I was grieving for Milt, and caring for my beautiful niece, a chance incident with my old bag made me realise that it was time to change my life, and my bag at the same time. That reorganising my bag was the first step to reorganising the way I did everything."

"I think that's something most women can relate to, and it seems to have been true!"

Ms West says she is pleased at the way the public have responded to Best Bag Ever, because she was told that it was a 'silly idea'.

She says this just goes to show that people should follow their dreams and not listen to their families or other people who might want to hold them back.

Ms West is candid about her past in West Auckland, where her family were involved in robbery and owned a second hand store which Ms West says was used to fence proceeds from the robberies.

"When you start at the bottom rung of the ladder of life, surrounded by crime", said the glamorous young businesswoman, "there's nowhere to go but up.""

"Growing up in a family of criminals, where stealing was a way of life, it would have been easy for me to get sucked into that world. Luckily I had the strength of will to escape, to find a moral path through life."

She says that seeing members of her family go to prison only strengthened her resolve to make a success of herself.

She puts some of this down to her philosophy which she describes as believing in the "beautiful positive".

"Having seen so many bad things in my life, it would have been easy for me to go with the hussy old negative but I've now seen there is a better way for me to live my life."

"What was so great about Milt was that he saw the positive in everyone, even my family, who were not very welcoming to him."

You can tell a lot about a girl from what's in her handbag …

Wallet
It has money in it. This is a thing it never used to have in it.

G-string
Spare undies are always handy. And they are clean!

Tampons, a bit fluffy
Ew. I would never use these, but they got trapped in the lining, okay?

Gambling chips
From Las Vegas, where I got married in a little chapel to my husband Milton Delaney III. And now I have so little left of Milt apart from his very generous bequest of $2.8 million.

Roach clip
It's there because it can be handy for clipping the tops of bags etc. Now, I don't use drugs anymore unless Munter is passing a joint round, or Van is. Or Van and Munter.

Pills of small unspecified type
They're not E, alright. They're probably vitamin pills or diet pills from when I was a model, before I got totally comfortable with the fact that I don't need to be a size 6 to be happy. Size 8 is just fine by me.

Business card
Another little bit of Milt and me, from my career in inspirational television.

Bottle opener
I was only looking after this for Van, who still thinks it's possible to open a bottle by using your eye socket. If you look closely he has the scars to prove it.

A message from Pascalle West

Okay, people have got very interested about what I have in my handbag, which is not surprising given that Best Bag is such a great idea and also that I have led such an interesting and inspirational life. And because I have given other people the Bag Life Challenge, it seems only fair that I am completely honest about my bag, the way it was Before. Because, yes ladies, it was a Sad Bag, with even a bit of Ho Bag thrown in. A bag and a life in desperate need of change. I'm not ashamed to share it with you.

Condoms
Let's face it, guys don't remember to carry these.

Mini-bar miniatures
I don't remember how these got here.

Painkillers
I always carry some because there are never any at home on account of my family always getting pissed and having hangovers.

Mobile phone

Make-up
None of these is from Bunser's the Chemist from the time things did fall into my boots. And if you want to get antsy about it, I have receipts!

Earring
I wish I could find the other one because these were given to me by my current fiancé Nicky Greegan, who is a lovely person and don't believe anything my family says about him.

Plasters
First aid is very important, especially when you are caring for the elderly, or your lovely niece, Jane, who has been mostly abandoned by her actual mother, and often her adopted mother too. It's a good thing that someone in this family cares.

Loretta's blog — defining moments

I, Loretta West, have started a blog. I didn't want to, given how lame blogs are, but I have to. It's a school thing that's to do with finding some way of channelling my antisocial behaviour. They said I should write about myself and 'my relationship with my family'. I'm related to them and I didn't have a choice in the matter, how much more does anyone need to know?

Starting with me. Loretta West. Some members of the extended West family (the police call them our 'associates') make the mistake of calling me Loretta Lynn on account of my Mum's inexplicable love of country music. They generally don't make the mistake twice. I'm 30 years of age but trapped in the body of a 15-year-old, which means I am trapped at school, but not for long.

Last year my dad, Wolfgang, who has a fine pedigree in thievery, managed to get himself incarcerated for 4 years. It sent Mum kind of mental and she delivered this fascist decree that from now on we keep on the straight side of the law. As if. For those of you that aren't familiar with my infamous family (i.e. you haven't been robbed by us), get a clue: we're infamous.

Since her brain explosion, Mum, or Cheryl if you like, has been trying her best to go straight. She's ended up with a lingerie business, Hoochie Mama. (Crotchless undies for fat West Auckland chicks — it makes me ill just typing those words.) Wolf spent most of his time doing his best to get out of jail so he could spare us this straight act of Mum's, which I'm pretty sure rips at his undies even more than ours. He's out now, on home detention, because this dodgy cop called Judd apparently framed him, even though Dad did actually do the crime.

As for the rest of my nearest and dearest, I may as well begin with my suck-up brother, Jethro, the family success story. He's this up-and-coming lawyer, upstanding and 100% up himself, even the 50 percent of him that pretends to be Maori so he can reap the benefits at his firm — all those tangata whenua dollars. Jethro happens to have an identical twin, Van. Identical in all but brains and not being an asshole. If ignorance is bliss then Van drifts through life (with his best mate, Munter) happily stoned, which he does anyway. Not that this stops him being a dork of the first order.

I have a sister called Pascalle. I call her 'Westward Ho' because she is one. She fancies herself as a model. I thought she was closer to her true calling when she worked as a stripper for a while (before Mum stopped her

— back to that 'going straight' thing). In between throwing herself at washed-up TV celebs and other knobheads, she spends her life on the couch, whining.

Theodore West, also known as Ted, also known as Grandpa, is about the only member of the West family I have much time for. He's this cool guy who was the greatest safecracker in New Zealand in his time. Now he's living with us because he burnt down his unit at the retirement village. Apparently he has Alzheimer's, but I reckon Grandpa still has heaps left up his sleeve.

As for yours truly, when I'm not trapped against my will in an educational asylum called Shadbolt High, I run a successful business empire called The Video Hut. The Video Hut specialises in pre-release DVDs on a cash-only-no-questions-asked basis. We **haven't** got *Sione's Wedding* because we believe in protecting local filmmakers (and we sold out). So that's me and my life for now. We're a pretty full-on family. We swear too much and we're not good at following what other people call 'rules' or 'the law' (despite what Mum believes in her deluded state). Welcome to my world.

Nothing says Happy Birthday like your parents rallying to ruin your life. Why is everything I do never enough?! My life is over.

ST MARY IGNATIUS SCHOOL FOR THE DAMNED
versus
WAIRARAPA: AUNT JEANETTE, HER FARM AND THREE LEATHER STRAPS AND CANE

I knew I got my evil from somewhere but how could Dad DO this? You gotta give it to him. Dad knows how to put up a fight, much like Ash in *Evil Dead II*. He may have the balls to chainsaw off his own hand while screaming, 'Who's laughing now?!', but you can't outsmart the Dead, and that is why I will win.
You don't have to be a man in the West family to pull a fast one, and you don't have to be one of my brothers to have a double. St Mary's will never see me coming.
Anyhow, my birthday turned out to be quite the success, heaps of presents, relief from Mum and Dad, and victory over the yardie. I never hurl.

http://www.outrageousfortune.co.nz/blog/

Death isn't funny.
There is nothing about death that is remotely funny.
Except there is. I'm sorry, but I can't help it. The bus she rode into was, apparently, a party bus. A bunch of pissed accountants out for an office party when Aurora rode a motorbike into them and died. There's a fucking night out for everyone concerned.
Oh, come on! Don't hate me for thinking that! There must be something funny about a party bus being involved in a fatal road smash. Or ironic at least.
But death isn't funny. So I find out.
Not when everyone in my house is walking round like they've just been hit on the head with a brick. Not when everyone is acting like a freakin' zombie, with no idea of what to say or do. Not when death just took away one of the few people on this planet I could actually give a shit about. Not when death sucks this much.

And sure as shit not when your brother is this train wreck, and I mean a complete freakin' train wreck. Van's mind has never been his strongest point, but I figure this is in serious danger of pushing him over the edge.
I don't think there's much you can do about death except hold on to the people who are alive.
How's that for pretty fucking profound?

Should you bvlog when you're pissed?
Hold on, that's not right. Blog. Blog. Blog. That's what I meant to type.
Should you blog when you're pissed? Probably not, but what the fuck I'm here and I have some shit I need to say. Like how Hayden Peters has a tiny penis.
I've been out with my stupid sister on some stupid night out getting pluc ked like a chicken.
I'm a bit drunk.
I said that, didn't I?
My brother Jethro is a wanker. Did I say that? He is. Bastard. Last time I saw him he wasleaving the bar with Bruce's sister draped all over him and some other chick. Ew.
Jethro is Hayden's only friend in the world. Not that he deserves friend
s because he's a horrible horrible person who I hate with all my heart.
He's a wanker and someone should stick a hose up his butt. Stick the whole fucking fire engine for all I care. Wanker too
I'm better than him. He has no right to do this to me. Screw him. I don't need him and it won't hurt tomorrow.
Hold om, someone just fell over in the hall.
It was Draska what a slut I should have kicked her as she crawlewd to van's room.
That gary guys okay. For a man. And all men are bastards.
I probably shouldn't post this right now, I should wait until the morning.
I feel less than ideal

Blog on Life

Bugger.
Shit.
Bugger.
Look, what do you want me to say? Yes, I'm pregnant. I'm that stupid slapper all those sanctimonious people talk about when they preach their 'It only takes one time' sermon. I cannot be a mother. I am not programmed to be a mother. I have too many other things I need to do with my life other than be a mother.
But I'm going to be a mother.
Shit.

———————————————

This is Pascalle West here. My sister doesn't know I am writing this blog but I am doing it for her own good because there is something anyone who reads her weird, mental ravings needs to know. My sister, Loretta West, is sick in the head.
So all I want to say is do not listen to anything Loretta says ever. She is evil in the way she can get people to do bad stuff for her and I am worried someone out there who isn't as emotionally centred as I am will fall under her spell.
So be warned. If you feel tempted to do anything Loretta suggests you should do, that you should think about all the tropical fish who were boiled alive thanks to her
You have been warned.

———————————————

When Pascalle and I were kids, we were this awesome shoplifting team. The way we'd work it was we'd go into a store, it didn't matter what store or if Mum or Dad or anyone else was with us, and we'd split up. Pascalle would then create a distraction. She was really good at distractions, because it made her the centre of attention and Pascalle loves being the centre of attention. Some things never change.
Anyway, sometimes she'd have a massive tantrum, sometimes she'd throw up (she was practising to be a model), sometimes she'd knock over a display stand (especially effective in supermarkets), sometimes she'd flash her knickers at the guys behind the counter. Once she even peed herself in Bunsen's the Chemist, which was a total act of devotion just to get the lip gloss I was meant to be stealing for her. (Pity I was laughing so hard I forgot to flog it.)
Anyway, while Pascalle was distracting I would take care of the business end of things. Man, we got away with heaps of stuff. Once I even walked out of the barbecue place with a three-burner barbecue plus gas bottle for Dad's birthday. Pascalle was stripping in a spa pool.
I guess the point here is that Pascalle has this ability to sail through life. She doesn't see the potential shit all around her and, somehow, the shit doesn't stick to her. The down-side of this is that she doesn't see the danger right in front of her — even if it is fucking obvious to everyone around her. Pascalle is deaf, blind and (especially) dumb, when it comes to anything outside her field of vision — a field of vision which extends, of course, only as far as 'me want, me get'.
She's gone now, has Pascalle. Left the loving arms of her Mother and family. Over to the other side. With Him.

School reports

Shadbolt High School
Report

Name: Jethro West

Subject: English – 7th Form

Teacher: Ms Caroline Darling

Form: 7A

Examination Mark: 78

Examination Median: 69

Close reading	Excellent
Speaking and listening in groups	Excellent
Essay Writing	Excellent

Participates and contributes in class	Always
Completes homework	Usually
Focuses on task	Always

Teacher comment:

In every way possible, Jethro is a joy to teach and to have around the classroom. He throws himself wholeheartedly into his work and rises to every challenge, often in unexpected but highly effective ways; and with a maturity that is surprising in one so young. In the future, I am sure Jethro will take every opening that comes his way and make every post a winning post.

NAME Loretta West

YEAR 1994

CLASS Year 1

LANGUAGE ORAL WRITTEN	Oral: Loretta is clearly a very bright child who could contribute more to class discussions than she currently does. When she does contribute she needs to learn to use less 'colourful' language and not to say things that make the other children cry. Efforts are continuing here. Written: Loretta is still stubbornly refusing to write, saying that in her family no one ever writes anything down in case it is used as evidence.
READING	Loretta is reading well above her age. In fact she often seems happiest when she is in a corner, with a book, away from the rest of the class.
HANDWRITING	The above re: her written language. EMD is the continuing.
MATHEMATICS	Loretta is clearly gifted with numbers, as witnessed by the lunchtime 'cookie-trading pyramid game' incident. She just needs to learn to apply her skills in a more constructive way.
PHYSICAL EDUCATION	Loretta enjoys running but still needs to learn to do more than just run away and off the school grounds. She is also very talented at the hiding part of Hide and Seek.
MUSIC MOVEMENT	Loretta could participate more in class singing, rather than tending to sit in the corner and glare.
ART	Loretta is a very gifted artist although she needs to work more on using colours other than black and drawing things other than owls that make the other children cry.
GENERAL COMMENT	Loretta is an intelligent and challenging pupil; she needs to work on her social skills, participating more in group activities and not biting members of staff.

CLASS TEACHER K.Shepherd   PRINCIPAL Bob Mc—   PARENT

Shadbolt High School
Report

Name:	Van West	**Year:**	1996
Class:	4th Form	**Form:**	4D

Grades: A Outstanding; B Very Good; C Average; D Below Average; E Very Poor

SUBJECT	GRADE	COMMENT
English Ms C Darling	D	Van needs to focus more on writing his work and less on writing notes to his friend Jared.
Mathematics Mr N Ward	D	Van has a limited understanding of basic numeracy and is trying hard to master multiplication and division.
Science Mr K Tremain	E	Lighting one's own farts with a Bunsen burner does not count as scientific experimentation, Van, it is just stupid. How many times do I have to tell you this?
Social Studies Ms J Wright	D	It would help Van immeasurably in this subject if he concentrated less on the 'social' and more on the 'studies'.
Art Ms H Marshall	E	Van approaches his artwork seriously but is limited by the fact he draws and paints only penises and breasts. Needs to broaden his focus.
Physical Education Mr I Goldingham	D	Capable of a lot more but severely under-motivated and lacking in comprehension of even the most basic of rules.
Latin Ms S Butler	E	I am convinced Van ended up in this class by mistake.

Dean:
J. Harris

Principal:
B Fordyce

NAME: Pascalle West **YEAR:** 1998 **CLASS:** Year 8

TOPICS: SCIENCE/SOCIAL STUDIES/HEALTH
Pascalle was an enthusiastic and willing student in our You and Your Body study. She shared herself generously with all the members of class and seemed to thoroughly enjoy the topic. Similarly her speech on the importance of growing was a highlight of that particular topic.

ART AND CRAFT:
Pascalle loves art and participates enthusiastically at all times, although the life modelling and body painting projects she undertook with several boys in the class perhaps stretched the boundaries of what was appropriate for intermediate art class.

CLASS MUSIC:
Pascalle is becoming a competent musician, especially on the triangle.

RECORDER:
Pascalle is still stubbornly refusing to join the rest of her class in the recorder orchestra on the grounds that it is a "huss" instrument that will damage her lips for modelling. The loud and phallic nature of some her jokes about the recorder are also a disruptive element in class.

PHYSICAL EDUCATION:
Pascalle very much enjoys physical education and takes a full part in all group sporting activities. She is not afraid to play contact sports, even with the boys in her class. Some of her alterations to the phys. ed uniform, however, leave a bit to be desired.

EXPLANATION OF ACHIEVEMENT GRADES:
1 — OUTSTANDING 3 — AVERAGE 5 — WELL BELOW AVERAGE
2 — VERY GOOD 4 — BELOW AVERAGE

ORAL LANGUAGE	EFFORT	A	ACHIEVEMENT	3
Pascalle is an enthusiastic speaker, never short of an opinion on anything. She needs, however, to learn to organise her thoughts more coherently, to be more concise in her speaking, and to not attack those who may question her views.				

WRITTEN LANGUAGE	EFFORT	C	ACHIEVEMENT	3
Pascalle has many ideas she wants to express but she needs to focus more on writing the actual words rather than drawing pictures of flowers to illustrate her work.				

HANDWRITING	EFFORT	B	ACHIEVEMENT	5
Pascalle needs to learn to not be in such a hurry to express her thoughts on paper as it renders her handwriting totally unintelligible.				

SPELLING	EFFORT	E	ACHIEVEMENT	5
Pascalle is still obstinately refusing to budge from her stated opinion that future supermarkets will need less spell- ther lebsility. To improve ate words, often by leaving out vowels altogether creates a whole new version of the English language.				

READING	EFFORT	D	ACHIEVEMENT	4
Pascalle is improving with her reading but still needs to work on reading more than just fashion and beauty magazines. She no longer needs to use her finger and read out loud when dealing with long sentences.				

MATHEMATICS	EFFORT	E	ACHIEVEMENT	5
Pascalle needs to understand that she will not have a modelling agent to do all that 'maths stuff' for her and that a basic comprehension of maths is important to enable her to survive in this world.				

EXPLANATION OF EFFORT GRADES:
A — EXCELLENT C — GOOD E — POOR
B — VERY GOOD D — FAIR

School reports

Wolfgang West: an interview

Many attempts were made to try to contact Wolf to ask him to contribute to this book but his whereabouts remained a mystery until, late in the piece, a young and intrepid editor finally made a breakthrough. What follows is a transcript of the phone conversation between Sebastian McDermott and Wolfgang West.

Wolfgang West (W) Yeah?
Sebastian McDermott (SM) Hello. Is that Wolfgang West?
W Who wants to know?
SM Hi, I'm Sebastian McDermott. I'm an editor from a publishing company. We're putting together a book about …
W Sebastian? You're yanking my chain?
SM What? No …?
W No one calls their kid Sebastian.
SM Well, ah …
W What's your real name?
SM Ah … it's … it is Sebastian.
(Silence)
W So what do you want?
SM We're compiling a book about…
W Is this a wind-up?
SM No …
W Are you a friend of bloody Eric's?
SM No.
W How did you get this number?
SM Well, ah, your son Van very kindly …
W Bloody Van. Jesus …
(Pause)
W Call me back on this number.

Sebastian is given an unusual phone number, which, using his investigative skills, he believes to be for a phone box in Kaikohe. He calls back.

W You took your bloody time.
SM Sorry, I was just … so you're up in Kaikohe?
(A dark silence pervades the phone line.)
W Well, well. Someone thinks they're a smart arse, don't they?
SM No, it's just a lot of people have been wondering where you are and … and … it's nice up in Northland, isn't it?
W Listen to me carefully. It's none of your goddamned business where I am. And if I was in Kaikohe — which I'm not — I wouldn't tell you. Got it?
SM No. I mean yes, no, I understand …

W But if you tell anyone that I am …
(A worrying pause.)

W Got a good dentist, Sebastian?
SM Honestly no, I'm sorry … I didn't mean to …
W What the hell do you want?
SM Right. Okay. Well. We're compiling a book about your family and were wondering if you'd like to contribute …
W A book?
SM Yes …
W So you are gay?
(Pause. Sebastian, being an advocate for the truth …)
SM Well, actually, as a matter of fact …
W I don't read books.
SM You don't have to read it. We need you to …
W Are you saying I can't read?
SM No!
W I can read pink-trouser boy. I can read bloody well. It's just that I choose not to read. I'm a busy man.

SM Of course. I understand.
W Contribute what exactly?
SM Anything. Your philosophy on life perhaps? Just a page or two …
W *(Laughing)* And you think I would write this down?
SM That would be great!
W Wests don't write shit down. Rule number one is, 'don't write shit down'. It will only come back to bite you on the arse like your dodgy neighbour's pitbull
SM You wouldn't have to write it down.
W Why the hell do you think I'd want to do this?
SM Well, people are interested in your family . .
W What business is my family to anyone else?
SM Well … your kids, Loretta, Van, Pascalle … have been helpful.
W Are you threatening my kids?
SM What? No! … No, I'm just saying …
W You leave my bloody kids out of this, all right?
SM Honestly, I'm in no way …
W Jesus, you people piss me off.
SM Look, I think we've got off on the …
W No! You listen to me. You come anywhere near my kids and I will personally reach down this phone and tear your throat out. You understand me?
(Sebastian swallows — hard.)
W You hear me?!
(Sebastian hangs up. A moment later his phone rings)

SM Um … hello?
W Isn't caller ID a wonderful thing, Sebastian?
SM Maybe.
W I've got your number. Literally. 09 378 … Gee, that wouldn't happen to be a Ponsonby number? And guess where I am, Sebastian?
SM Ah …
W Not in fucking Kaikohe …
(Sebastian hangs up and footsteps can be heard hurrying out of the room.)

Sebastian was last heard of boarding a plane to Sydney, where he apparently found work in a club just off Oxford St. But don't tell Wolf that, for Christ's sake.

THE 7 DEADLY VAN AND

What are you most proud of?
VAN   Apart from my success with the ladies, I can burp all 24 letters of the alphabet. That's a pretty good talent to have, especially at parties.
JETHRO   Ever since I was a kid, I have had this ability to talk my way out of anything. Back then I used to blame Van for everything, now I don't even need to do that.

What brings out the green-eyed monster in you?
VAN   Not that I'm jealous of my dork brother, but I used to wish he was the one who got into trouble, not me.
JETHRO   I don't get jealous. Jealousy is for losers.

What was the last luxury item you splashed out on?
VAN   Does a great big bag of Te Puke Thunder count?
JETHRO   In my family you never let on when you've bought anything, because our sister Loretta will steal it.

What's your favourite food?
VAN   The chicken burritos at the Mexican place run by the Korean family just down the road from where the Lucky Dollar store used to be. And Mum's fish pie.
JETHRO   Mum's fish pie. And cheese.

SINS OF JETHRO WEST

When are you at your laziest?
VAN   What's the difference between lazy and just chilling out?
JETHRO   Sunday. I figure if it's good enough for God, it's good enough for me.

When was the last time you lost your temper?
VAN   I don't like anger. It scares me. If you have an anger problem, you should try Te Puke Thunder.
JETHRO   Probably the last time I spoke to a member of my family, that usually does it.

Who or what do you lust after?
VAN   Hayley Westenra. Some people say that is wrong but I can't help it.
JETHRO   Lust is such an uncool emotion. I s'pose if you forced me to answer I might say Kate Moss. Yeah, I could go there.
VAN   And she has no taste in men, so you might have a chance.
JETHRO   Hey! Get out of my question, loser!
VAN   Bite me.

Ted West's guide to gambling

Right then. Someone asked if I would give some tips on the gee gees. Bottom line is Wests don't write things down. It will only come back and bite you where it hurts quicker than a dodgy curry through the lower colon. However with something as important as the gee gees I'm prepared to make an exception so I've borrowed Loretta's lapdog thingie here and am giving this typing lark a go. Talk about bloody slow and ∆∆∆∆∆∆∆∆∆∆∆∆∆∆∆∆∆∆∆∆∆∆∆∆∆∆∆∆∆∆∆∆∆∆∆∆ happened there and ∆∆∆∆∆∆∆∆ shit don't know what the hells happening•ª§§¢¢™®†ƒ¨¨'æ… æ˙≥≤∆˚©¬§†ø®ƒ©∫jesus!

Right then. That seems better. Hang on got to take a slash.

Right you are. There have been a lot of methods touted over the years. So I'll let you in on a few.

Dumping
A bloke I knew by the name of Jim 'Bum' Trumich was always fascinated by the contents of his bowel in the bowl. A bit like reading tea leaves if you like. He swore by this method and would eat a lot of prunes before a big race day. If he managed to get one to curl round on itself he knew he could pick a winner. Reckons he came out ahead over the years but the colostomy bag put an end to that method. Poor bugger.

Farting
Then there was old Mary O'Donnagal. Lovely girl but terrible problem with wind. She used to involuntarily let rip like a machine gun. Usually when she was getting up off the barstool. But never one to feel embarrassed — she saw it as sign. Whatever the number she'd take it and put it on to win. Over the years of course she lost everything and she drinks sherry out the back of the New Lynn shops now.

Dogs
Don't waste your time with the greyhounds. Any animal stupid enough to run hell for leather around a track chasing a dead, fluffy animal is not worth betting on. Where is the intelligence? Where is the art born from man riding beast? There is something truly magnificent about a racehorse in motion which reminds me …

The love of a good horse
A jockey I heard of, Ernie Tonks, took that notion to an extreme. Fell in love with a horse he rode a lot. Hung up his saddle and moved into the paddock with Driving Miss Daisy. True he did. Gave away his worldly possessions to live with the filly. Couldn't stop marvelling at her magnificent haunches. Of course a lot of people thought he was porking the old mare but this was an outrageous accusation. It wasn't physically possible for a start. Being a jockey he'd have needed a step ladder. And he'd given that away with everything else.

Right. Just got to drop the kids off at the pool — be right back.

Well that was a bit overwhelming. I'd give it 10 minutes if I were you. Now where was I? Oh, right —

The Formula

There is of course the magic equation. This was popular in the early 80s and was touted as a sure-fire scientific solution. It goes something like this.

Horse weight times the jockey weight = 625 x 52 divided by the number of horses in the race times the number of wins over the last three years (substitute wins for places if it's had none and minus 20 from final total) divided by the race number on the day plus 1 for a wet track, 2 for a soft track and 3 for hard track.

The total will give you the guaranteed placing in any race. For example:

Golden Shower running at Te Rapa in the 3.10

Actually bugger this I'll grab a pencil …

$$625 \times 52 = \frac{32500}{15}$$

$$= 2167 \times 4$$

$$= \frac{8668}{5} = \frac{1734}{} + 2$$

$$1736$$

Then you drop a decimal point in because you can do that in maths. It becomes 17.36. So you can see Golden Shower would come seventeenth in a field of 15 so what a load of tosh that turned out to be. But many good men went mad in the 80s filling in Mighty Jotter Pads trying to get it right.

Me? I use more instinctive methods. As far as they go … well, you can all bugger off. Why would I tell you?

On the other hand, if you can meet down the Rusty Nail and buy me a port and lemon I'll give you the inside on the 2.20 at Addington.

P.S. just so you know this took me three and half days to type so I hope you're bloody satisfied ∂∂∂∂∂∂∂∂∂∂∂∂   ∂∂∂∂∂∂∂∂∂∂∂∂∂∂∂∂∂∂∂∂   ∆∆∆∆∆∆∆∆∆∆∆∆∆∆∆∆∆∆∆∆∆shit}{}{}}}}ΩΩΩΩΩ}}|||| christ, bugger!

The Tool Guy Code

1. Don't park on a sloping driveway if your handbrake is dodgy.
2. Do not attempt to eat a pie and talk on a cell phone and use a Skil saw at the same time. A gud pie deserves proper attention. Also, you might drip hot pie on your hand and that can really sting.
3. Always charge GST cos if you don't, Loretta gets real mad.
4. Some GST numbers are easy like the GST on $200 is $25.00. This is an easy one to remember.
5. But even if you can't work out what the GST is supposed to be just make it up. Like for instance, if a job is only worth $76 it's impossible to know what the GST is on $76 so make the job $200. Likewise, if a job costs $376 the GST on that is way, way too hard so just round it down to $200.
6. Where possible, charge jobs out at $200 plus GST.
7. Unless of course the client offers a 'cashie' in which case a simple hundy is sweet as a nut. Just DON'T TELL LORETTA!
8. Try not to take a dump in people's houses if they're home, cos a lot of people get a bit 'thingy' if tradesmen stink out their house. It's better to do it outside behind a bush or something and cover it over. People appreeshiate that sort of consideration.
9. But make sure it's not their vege garden.
10. Always have a bog roll in the glove box.
11. Try not to perv at clients as they're explaining the job they want you to do — even if they're quite hot and have a really nice rack.
12. And don't perv at their butts as they're walking away because — every time a coconut — they turn around and catch you out.

13. And don't undress them with your mind. This is easy to do when they're super hot but a dangerous activity to indulge in because ...
14. Some clients are men. And if you've had a lunchtime spliff you can start to involuntarily undress them as well and that can get pretty freaky.
15. Avoid intercourse with clients.
16. Not even pashing. Not even if they're really up for it and offering a 'no strings' scenario. Not even if they're super hot and offering 'the big kahuna'. It will only end badly and make you feel professionally compromised. (Sometimes even used.)

17. If you do happen to accidentally find yourself in the root position with a hot client, do not accept money. This makes you a male ho bag.
18. If you do axidentally accept money, don't forget the GST. (Although it's way better if it's a cashie — then always buy beers with it for your mates so you don't feel so guilty.)
19. The one exception is that you may have 'auto-rooted' (which is when you do something that you can't remember cos you were too mashed up but your body carries on with sense memory). This can happen in theory but has yet to be proven 100%. But when in doubt (if you are caught with your pants down) blame the 'auto-root' and all will be forgiven — once. Twice is pushing it and three times you're just a dirty dog who is using the Tool Guy brand to get laid.
20. Always remember the code.

VAN   Munter

Munter's guide to a gud time

I bin asked to share something important about life and I just wanted to say that life to me is really important.

I thought about talking about frendship like with my best mate Van becoz he's real important but so is Kasey and so where do you stop and not ofend people?

So I decided on revealing a secret secret about how to find tru happiness — or Tru bliss as we used to say until there was that band that came along with all those hot chicks. (None of them were anywhere as hot as Kasey tho — for the rekord.)

So here's what I know and I want to share the knowledge so that others can know what I know about the important things in life and let happiness abound. And this is it.

(Achaly — when I first sent this in they said there was some words I couldn't use coz this is like a book and when you write things down it's differunt to just saying it at the pub and people can get in truble and stuff and I don't want no truble for no one. Thes enuf truble in this world you know what I'm saying so I had to change a few words to make the world a happier place. Peace out)

My mums freaky cookie recipe which is the best freaky cookie recipe ever

The thing with freaky cookies is that its all about the ingredients. The ingredients have to be just right. When they're right they can bring on perfection and the perfect freaky cookie is a rare thing these days.

This is a recipe handed down from my uncle Carlos to my Mum and to me. Now it can be yours.

You need <u>flower</u> — not any of this hippie brown wheatmeal flower. Just white flower from the dairy is gud. But if your out of it when you goes to the dairy be careful not to get cornflour by mistake otherwise you end up gluing up your insides for days.

You end up with a real bad butt plug. That happened to Van once and Cheryl had to get out the garden hose but … yeah … you don't really need to know about that. Anyways …

And butta. And normal buttas what you want. Definitely not one of them butta substitutes 'cos I saw this documentary the other day and you wouldn't believe what's in some of them. One scientist reckoned some have up to 90% petro-chemical additifs.

Eat enough of that shit and one slip of the lighter round the cone and **BAM** you could become a spontaneous fire eater! (Then again this scientist was wearing a raincoat with the hoody up and roman sandals with socks so…you know.)

But anyways butta, yeah and flower and:

sum melty peanut butta for flava
sum white suga
sum brown suga
½ teaspoon baking soda or baking powder or maybe both — yeah both I reckun
A squirt of vanila essense (get the imitation one — its way cheaper. And actually it's free sometimes 'cos those tiny bottles often fall into your pocket when your in those crowded aisles of the dairy. If you want advice about this Pascalle West is the xpert.)
1 large egg (that's from a chicken — not Aaron Spiller)
And of course you need the magic ingredient that puts the freak into the freaky.
<u>A cup load all ground up</u>

This is so not true and those things really did fall into my boots. P.

Despite what heaps of people say don't put primo stuff in your cookies. And if you grind it up in a coffee grinder this way you can set some aside for Tea. That tea is real nice — speshally gud for relaxing just before bed cos it gives you ace dreams.

My dreams are usually about Chryslers and fish and going to Real Big Doobie Land where everything is made out of joints and hash and everyone is real chilled and Beyonce is there with Kasey and their both into it and that's one of those recurring dreams but … oh yeah …

So you set aside the ground up stuff for tea and mix half of the rest in with the flower. So you have real 'speshal' flower now. Choice eh?!

The other half you gently simmer with the butta. How many halves is that? Doesn't matter, just use heaps.

Munter's guide to a gud time

The best cabbage comes from my Uncle Carlos. Hes always holding heaps of primo sorts from top of the range but like I sed, I can't say from where — altho he does spend heaps of time down in Te Puke and he always comes back real amped from the Naki. If you want to find him he's always down at the pub but I can't say which one 'cos then he'll get busted so achaly you'll have to find your own.

Next you need to figure out a way for the butta to mix with the ground up stuff using heat and a pan. Then mix this speshal butta mixture with the peanut butta with all the suga, brown suga, baking soda and baking powder. Then beat in the egg and vanilla. Then the speshal flower and all the other stuff and make it into a doe.

(Oh, make sure you use a bowl for all this — it's just better that way otherwise it ends up all ova the floor.)

Put the doe on a greased tray in the oven. Then you can make one really big cookie for speshal ocashions or lots of little cookies. You can use a fork to make designs on the doe like smiley faces are gud.

Then you put them in the oven on hot for bout 10 minutes. Make sure the oven is actually on. Sometimes if you've bin licking the spoon and the bowl too much you can get quite distracted and forget stuff like that. It's real disappointing when you cum bak later and theres no cookies only doe.

Of course the thing with my Mum's cookies is you gotta take them one at a time or else — well, if they come out real strong and you overdo it you can end up with a full 'freaky cookie body coma' and bad shit can happen. It happened to me once and I really don't wanna go there …

And once this guy I know Horse Berensen got really mashed up on a big cookie and went to his own stag party and shaved off his own pubes. So you really hav to be careful.

But eat and be merry. May happiness abound. Peace out.

Munter

Wayne Judd

Incident report
12 June 2000
3.43 a.m.

This evening Constable Hickey and myself were called to an incident at a house at John Mulgan Street. This house is apparently well known to the West Auckland CIB. In this instance, a Noise Control Officer had been called three times and had confiscated the stereo causing the offending noise. Much to his dismay, a second stereo was brought in to play and the noise had resumed. He and his associate confiscated that, but a third stereo was produced.

This game of cat and mouse continued three more times. The endless supply of stereos can only be attributed to the fact that one Wolfgang West runs a secondhand appliance shop, which is suspected to be how the family and associates fence stolen goods.

When I arrived, I found the said Noise Control Officer in a very distressed state. He was in tears and mumbling incoherently. When asked if he had been threatened by Wolfgang West, he said he was more scared of a dark-haired girl of around ten years of age. The man was clearly confused.

Upon entering the West premises we were confronted by a scene of drunken mayhem.

A beer bong had been manufactured in the backyard, reportedly by Theodore West, who is also known to police. It consisted of several hosepipes and the radiator from a Falcon V6 suspended from the rotary clothesline. Several guests were passed out on the grass beneath this contraption. This was one of the more reckless cases of alcohol abuse I have seen.

Hickey and I attempted to break up a particularly vicious fight between a woman named Rochelle and a teenager called Corinna that was the result of a dispute over a man named Horse. We were told to, 'Fuck off and mind our own business,' as it was a personal matter, and if they wanted the cops involved they would have, 'Fucking well asked for it.' With that the eye gouging continued as we were distracted by two teenagers by the names of Munter (real name Jared Mason?) and Van West (of same address), who were discovered playing do or dare by squirting the garden hose at overhead power lines. This level of stupidity is probably the most moronic I've witnessed.

The noise was finally contained when it was apparent that the alcohol supply had run dry. Despite all the abusive language, only two arrests were made.

A man by the name of Eric — reputedly an uncle — was apprehended on the neighbour's property wearing women's underwear, allegedly taken from the same neighbour's clothesline. This associate of the Wests has convictions for burglary, receiving and DIC, and works at the West Galleria.

One Mule Berensen, 26, of Stead Crescent, was arrested for indecent exposure. He was discovered semi-naked by Constable Hickey, in the front garden, fondling the remains of a rotisserie chicken.

It is clear to me that this family and their associates will be a regular and unfortunate feature of my duties in West Auckland. They are reportedly responsible for a considerable percentage of crime in the region.

Detective Wayne Judd

NB: Cheryl West, wife of Wolfgang, threatened to lay a complaint about police harassment and demanded my rank and number. I gave her my necessary contact details.

Tips on living with the Wests

I used to be a cop. That is no secret — as Ted will joyfully remind anyone within five seconds of meeting them. I'm not ashamed of it. I was a pretty good one, I reckon. Tried to be fair. But when I joined the force, had one of my colleagues said, 'One day you'll be shacked up with the West family,' I probably would have a) said, 'Say that again and knock that smirk off your face,' and b) given them one on the jaw in the locker room anyway for being a shit stirrer.

But life is no straight line and it has a funny way of changing your world view when you least expect it. That incident report someone dug out (on the other page) is an example of that I guess. Hey, I'm not too proud to admit when I'm wrong. So, for whatever crazy reason that might come up where you find yourself living with the Wests, here are a few pointers.

Grandpa

When he's not urinating on you from the balcony or calling you a 'Porky Trotsky trotter face pig features,' for the ninth time in half an hour, Ted's okay — so long as you agree with him. But then if you do, he'll change his tune just to be contrary. Get used to it and don't bother fighting it. Let it wash over you (it's better than what's streaming out of his bladder).

And one other small but important piece of advice: should you see Ted leaving the toilet ahead of you, turn around, make a cup of tea, sit down and give it a good ten minutes (actually 15 is much, much safer).

Loretta

As long as you don't believe a word she says until you have considered all angles, Loretta can be fun to be around. She's a very smart young lady. Just watch your wallet and if you hear a scratching sound coming from your glovebox first thing in the morning — don't open it. I did. Once.

It was back when I first started seeing Cheryl. A terrorised stoat screeched out and leapt down the front of my shirt. Sure it was a message and sure I took it on board and then chose to completely ignore it. (By the way I've never said this but, 'Fuck you, Loretta — I'm still here!') But that's Loretta's style. Why say it to your face when you can park a feral animal in a person's private space and let it do the talking?

Van

Never enter Van's room unless you absolutely have to. But, should there be a lack of clean crockery in the kitchen it can probably be found in Van's room (not clean, however). Should you find yourself in there, avoid all used tissues, scrunched up T-shirts and discarded undies like The Plague. They probably are. The crockery is usually found under the bed and will harbour large, blue-and-black furry bits. If you look closely these are actually moving but are not small pets.

On first impressions it's easy to think that Van is slightly retarded. He's not. But there was something about a freezer when he was young and that was true. But let's just say a big brain is not as cool as a big heart. Van has a heart big enough to pump the lifeblood around most of West Auckland. Be good to Van and you'll get it back in spades.

Munter

Not strictly a West but he is one in all but name. As long as Munter has a good supply of weed he's a happy guy. He's a thinker. He once told me he managed to think of four different things at once. He called it 'mental multi-tasking' but when he went for five he lost it all and has no memory of any of the thoughts except that he thinks it was 'a sunny day with the sun really shining.'

I jokingly suggested he might want to become an air traffic controller. That's a multi-tasking job. Munter got pretty excited. He thought that was 'an awesome idea'. He reckoned getting really stoned and guiding in planes would be 'pretty out there with all those freaky, blinking lights on the radar'. Thankfully, I think he lost track of the idea and never organised a job interview.

Pascalle

A lot of people take Pascalle the wrong way. They think because of the way she dresses and talks and sleeps around that she's a slut. Actually, she's not (water polo team and the First XV aside — but that's ancient history). In fact, once she gives someone her heart she is fiercely loyal.

However, loyalty will quickly evaporate if you don't treat certain containers in the fridge with the greatest caution and utmost respect. What may look like curry paste or hummus could well be Pascalle's latest skin rejuvenation concoction and woe betide anyone who spreads that on their Huntly and Palmers. Also, the last four inches of a cucumber must always remain sacred. She still likes to do that freaky thing on her eyes.

Jethro

Yeah. Jethro. Jethro is … Jethro. And he really loves his mum. So he and I perhaps have too much in common there.

And speaking of whom, have I forgotten anyone? Oh, yeah … the reason I got involved with this crazy family in the first place …

Cheryl

If you choose to pick a fight with Cheryl be prepared to lose (even if you think you haven't) because it will feel that way.

Maybe to the outside world Cheryl can come across as a hard-arsed woman. Put it this way, I've heard it said that there is nothing more terrifying than being in the Alaskan woods and being confronted by a grizzly bear. When they stand up on their hind legs and stare down at you, your bowels well and truly open up. That said, when Cheryl barrels up to you clutching her handbag, gripping her car keys and stabbing a finger in your face while tearing shreds off you — well, let's just say — I've seen grown men break down and weep.

Shit, don't get me wrong. She can piss me off at times. She can drive me nuts with her stubbornness and her black-and-white point of view on matters that are definitely grey. But I love her — always have and reckon I will till the end of time. Can't imagine anything that could change that. Yeah. Love ya, Cheryl.

P.S. Wolf — wherever the hell you are — no hard feelings, fella. You're most welcome to call in for a barbie or a roast anytime. I'll be the one at the head of the table, carving the meat.

A neighbour speaks

I have been living next door to the Wests for a while now. There's the Wests on one side, the Borsiches on the other and next to them is a flat. (People are in and out of there like nobody's business and I think they're on the P.)

I got this place after I split with my ex-de facto, Tipene-the-builder. He's not the father of Sharonne or Tarin. He said he loved me because of my bubbly personality and natural curves.

Oh yeah, was I sucked in!

Turned out he was mostly after the settlement I got from Greg-the-electrician. After the courtcase with Tipene, this was the only place I could get.

I see a whole lot of stuff in our street. By this you might think I am nosy, but I just happen to notice what people have in their recycling. It really pisses me off the way the Wests stick their bottles into mine because they don't have enough room in theirs. God, the drinking that goes on next door, and they never invite you over.

And I never went through theirs to see if there was any left in the bottom of a bottle, which is what that nasty old man next door said. This while he was hanging his dick over the balcony and pissing into the garden! Honestly.

I'm a person too, but you don't see them next door giving me any sympathy, even after the hysterectomy. Her next door thinks she's God's gift, always strutting round in her heels and her low-cut fancy tops. I'm not a slag for wearing a dressing gown, it's just a lot more comfortable after the surgery.

And the thing with the washing just got blown out of proportion. I wasn't stealing from their line. I was just getting things in because it was raining and I thought they weren't there and so yes, a couple of fancy tops ended up with my stuff. But Sharonne, my daughter, wears those kinds of things, so it was completely understandable.

And I don't sticky beak, whatever she says next door. I'm just outside a lot because I like fresh air, when I'm smoking so I don't affect Tayla, who is my granddaughter, who lives with us since Tarin is at Ways of Light, which is, yes, an addiction and P programme.

Her next door has gone `straight'. You wouldn't credit the number of TVs and stereos that used to go into that place, especially when Wolf was there. And the cops were doing nothing! And they are a mean lot next door, especially the young one, Loretta. I'm fairly sure it was her who ran over our cat one day, but she denied it. If she's that mean to animals, think of what she'd do to a person!

Wolf was alright. He used to give me the eye. I had his number, with his shorts and his tight sexy T-shirts and how he'd walk around naked after he'd had a shower. (I only know this because the lights were on next door and not because I was watching.)

But he was buff and taut and screaming sex, sex, sex. But her next door went and dumped him. Then he was back for a bit, and then there was a lot of throwing of crockery. (They must be made of money over there the way they throw plates around.) And then he left town, ground down by her bossiness.

And now, she's got another one. Wayne, with excellent abs and a taut butt, which I only know because they don't pull the curtains and not because I was looking, but also because of a flyer at the Rusty Nail that said he had a swimmer's body. (Sharonne thinks he did the Commonwealth Games but I said she was talking through a hole in her patuzi.)

I've always had a thing for guys with the natural suntan (hence mistake with T'pene-the-builder). And they often go for me on account of my bubbly personality and natural curves. And sometimes, when he's putting out the recycling or getting the paper, Wayne gives the eye, oh yes he does. I reckon it would be all on, if her next door wasn't there ...

Not that I take an unnatural interest in what goes on next door, because I have heaps and heaps going on in my own life.

As I say to Sharonne, I could write a book about it, or even a movie.

Department of Social Welfare report: Nicky and Sheree Greegan

Department of Social Welfare

This evening I was called, with my supervisor, to an incident at Baxter Bay, outside Whakatane. Two children had been apprehended living in a bach. They had stolen food and alcohol. The children were found sleeping in the same bed.

The older of the siblings, Sheree G., aged 14, would not speak to police about the death of her stepfather, Michael R. His death had already been ruled as due to natural causes; he had aspirated his own stomach contents.

My supervisor believes that Sheree was involved, but this could not be concluded from the autopsy. I was upset by his attitude to Sheree.

When I spoke to Sheree she was angry and withdrawn. I get the strong feeling she had been abused by her stepfather, Micheal R., although she would not disclose this.

She was mostly upset that her brother, Nicky G., aged 12.8, was to be taken into custodial care because of incidents with police. Sheree has promised that he will never come to police attention again. He has also said the same thing to me.

I believe that they should be kept together given their traumatic circumstances.

The children have been neglected by their mother, Sharon G., who has issues with alcohol. Two years ago she abandoned them. They have been living with Micheal R., a beneficiary, since then.

The children are clearly mature for their years and also intelligent, despite considerable neglect/abuse. The only familial attachment or loving relationship they have is to each other.

My supervisor feels that the children should be separated, but I strongly feel this will not facilitate their development.

When I questioned Sheree about the shared bed, she claimed that this was normal for them. Her brother has been upset since the departure of their mother. She clearly cares for him deeply; I question the wisdom of splitting up these siblings at this time!

I am concerned that Sheree will not complete her schooling and may become promiscuous as a result of sexual abuse. I fear for the long-term consequences here, but I have been overruled by my supervisor.

I have to wonder if I have what it takes to be a social worker, especially when my views are rarely considered.

I may take a job at The Warehouse instead.

Lorraine Matangi
Trainee social worker.

(Lorraine Matangi took a job at a local vineyard where she used her people skills as Sales Manager. She married Terry, who is in roofing, and they have three children. She is very involved in junior soccer. From time to time she still worries about what happened to Nicky and Sheree ...)

Letter to the editor

Dear Outrageous Fortune book bosses,

Why you write bloody book about no good West family?
Why you waste paper on those bloody thieving Wests?
Why you not write book about people who do good, not bloody criminals?

Let me tell you something about bloody West family. They are no good. They are sort of people who call you friend to your face, then plunge knife in when you turn your back, then steal the watch your grandfather gave you as you lie on the ground bleeding. They are criminals, plain and simple. They say, 'No, we are not criminals any more,' but when you put lipstick on a pig it is still a pig.

When my beautiful daughter Draska meets the Wests, she is a young virgin, until that seronja Van West, he take advantage of her. He make her do the sort of disgusting things my wife would never do to me. Then when he finish having his wicked way with her, he throw her away like old pair of shoes. She still carries emotional scars to this very day so that no decent Croatian boy will touch her.

We have high hopes when she become married to Paulie Janovic, the panelbeater's son, but he was so disgusted when he found out the sort of depraved things the Wests teach Draska to do, that he leave town. And all stories that say he leave because he find her in bed with his brother Stevie are lies put about by those stinking Wests!

Why you write book about thieves and criminals and perverters of innocent girls? Why you not write book about Croatian community and the many fines works they do? My son, Slavko, he has won Golden Accordion, symbol of national accordion supremacy, two time in a row — why you not write book about him?

My beautiful wife and I hope the Wests and all who support them fail and their children grow up ugly and unwed. .

Yours sincerely,

Tomislav Doslic

West associates: where are they now?

The Hongs
Previous employers of Van West. Suzy Hong had intimate relations with the twins.

Mr and Mrs Hong are happily ensconced in Hong Kong where Jasmine is now at preschool. Her baby brother, Xavier, is already showing early signs of great intelligence and an uncanny ability to deflect blame for his bad behaviour on to others, usually his sister. This both intrigues and disconcerts Mr Hong. Mr Hong is keen to return to New Zealand at some stage. Suzy Hong is not.

Tracy Hong
Former girlfriend of Jethro West.

Tracy is living in Sydney where she is playing hard-to-get with an investment banker. She owns an art gallery in Oxford Street and, although she knows nothing about art, this has not stopped her from being very successful due to her understanding of style and how people prefer paintings that are either ugly or match their décor.

Eric
Known as Uncle Eric though no direct relation to the West family. Friend of Wolf.

Gee — who the hell knows? Presumed to still be in hiding somewhere and doing a very good job of it. It would be nice to hear from him soon.

Corky
The West family lawyer until he began a love affair with methamphetamine.

Franklin Cork was recently paroled. Due to his horticultural tendencies he has settled into a Hawke's Bay lifestyle and is planning to grow olives and grapes. In addition, he has recently opened a rustic homestay in an ex-shearer's quarters not far from Paul Holmes' place. You can email him at corky@myhawkesbayholiday.com. Corky was recently reunited with his best friend Owen (his peace lily).

Caroline Darling
Teacher at Shadbolt High and Jethro's lover while he was at school.

Caroline is relishing her role as Deputy Principal of a private boys' school in Dunedin. Though busy with administrative tasks, she still finds time to keep her hand in at the coalface and insists on taking classes in a relieving role. She mainly teaches English, though occasionally biology. The students rate her as a most excellent and exciting teacher.

Kurt
Loretta's co-worker at the Video Hut.

Kurt is trying to put his criminal past behind him. He is a junior account manager at an up-and-coming advertising firm, channelling his hatred at Loretta by making as much money as possible. He directed the recent anti-drink-driving advert where a young man falls asleep at the wheel and knocks over a young woman in blue jeans and a black T-shirt as she steps out of a video rental place. This particular ad has been nominated for many awards and has been cited for its gritty realism.

Glenn Hickey
Former sidekick to Wayne Judd when he was in the police force.

Glenn left the police force moments before he was pushed. Though he had dreams of working as a private eye or for the Secret Service as an agent, his proclivity for being distracted by women's underwear has found him running his own laundromat in Howick. Should you be in Howick and need special attention, especially for your delicates, Glenn is an expert.

Corrina Balani
School friend of Pascalle's, renowned for her 'ho'-ness and many children.

Corrina is pregnant with her sixth child. Dane Harris denies paternity this time. So does Mule Berensen, The Raj, Horse Berensen and The Gooch. Aaron Spiller has put his hand up, but no one believes him. Corrina is considering selling this one to the Colquhouns as well, but she'll up the price this time.

Gary Savage
Wolf's half-brother.

Gary may or may not be in Australia. He may or may not be co-owner of a new mine 800 km northeast of Perth. He may or may not spend time in Asia, where he has a holiday home (not in his name). He may or may not have recently returned to New Zealand under a false name and been making enquiries about purchasing a property in Kumeu. The property is apparently in good condition, though the driveway may need some work.

Danielle
Jethro's ex-girlfriend, and former wife of Gary.

Danielle is living in Nelson with Robbie to be nearer to her parents. She is no longer using the name Savage and has reverted to her maiden name. She never received the hundred grand she was owed by Gary and has had no contact with Jethro. Danielle has sworn off men, who 'only treat you badly, break your heart and rip you off' and is currently involved with a woman called Skye, whom she met while cooking in a wholefoods cafe. As a result, Danielle has fallen out with her parents.

Monica Judd
Wayne Judd's ex-wife.

Monica has not been happy in West Auckland for some time and is considering a transfer. She's tossing up between the Manawatu and Taranaki, or anywhere with good hunting opportunities. She completely denies that her desire for a transfer has anything to do with her 'having a thing' for the hunky new detective sergeant in her office. She was in no way angry when he rebuffed her advances and kind offers to show him the smooth action of her Ruger. Monica is also in no way behind the rumour that the new DS with his tight T-shirts and natty shades is probably gay.

Loretta West
As is her name by deed poll. Formerly known as Jools.

Loretta was an intern on a major international feature film shot in Wellywood, where she worked hard on the unit table and came to the director's attention because of the quality of her fruit and yoghurt breakfasts. She also attended several short film festivals with her first short film, *Jandal*. This was followed by a second short film, *Thong*, and after more festivals she is now considered 'one to watch'. As a result of talent, hard work and intensive networking at the Matterhorn, Loretta/Jools has a feature in development. It is the gruelling tale of a young girl growing up in a dysfunctional family in a moody rural landscape. To date the film has had enthusiastic feedback for its dark themes and haunting images.

The official Outrageous Fortune trivia quiz

1. What was the name of Grandma Rita's comforting, cricket-playing chum?
2. On which birthday is it traditional for the Wests to drink the yard?
3. Which department store was Grandpa robbing in the famous —— cock-up?
4. What was the location of Cheryl and Wolf's first root?
5. What is Falani's wife's name?
6. What did the West family give Cheryl for her birthday in Series 1?
7. What was Aurora's surname?
8. What is the name of the shop Van used to manage?
9. Mrs Hong has a daughter. What is her name?
10. What is the name of Jethro's first teacher and lover?
11. What was the occupation of the man Loretta lost her virginity to?
12. The guy who Loretta lost her virginity to might be recognisable as which character on *Shortland Street*?
13. Eric had a son. His name?
14. Who did Eric get lucky with at his son's funeral?
15. The Wests all attended the same illustrious high school (except when Loretta went Catholic). The name of the high school is?

Question 5

Question 7

16. There were two Loretta Wests and one of them made a short film. What was the title of that film?
17. What is Munter's real name?
18. Who usually supplies the dope for Munter's mum's famous dope cookies?
19. Name Wayne Judd's ex-wife.
20. When Monica asked Wayne if he wanted to 'go bush', what was she proposing?
21. What was the council lady's name?
22. What did Loretta save at Tutaekuri Bay?
23. What was the name of Vern Gardiner's commune?
24. What was Aurora's song?
25. What was the name of the gang that Van saved Aurora from?
26. What did Lloyd stab the billboard with?
27. What is Sparky's real name?
28. What is the name of the wannabe gang that attacked Wolf?
29. What was the name of the backyard-cricket ball he threw at them?
30. How many people has Loretta slept with?

Question 26

31 If the question posed by Loretta is, 'Who ate all the pies?', what is the answer?
32 Cheryl has how many sisters?
33 What are their names?
34 Wolf never gambles. True or false?
35 Draska faked her pregnancy by obtaining urine from who?
36 In Episode 1 the family had a business. What was it called?
37 Loretta tried to sell her baby to a wealthy couple. Where do they live?
38 What did Van want to call Baby Jane?
39 But what was Judd's suggestion?
40 What film was Baby Jane named after?
41 Name the two famous actresses who played lead roles in the film? (1 point for each)
42 According to Grandpa, where is Leon Shuker buried?
43 What is the name of the low-rent bar Pascalle briefly worked at?
44 What is the name of Aaron Spiller's tow truck?
45 What is the title of Grandpa's favourite prison-themed porno film?

46 In the infamous job that netted the krugerrands, name Grandpa's old crew.
47 Why was Lefty called Lefty?
48 Name the coveted jewel that Grandpa stole for Ngaire.
49 What did he steal from the Croatian Society?
50 What was the name of the law firm where Jethro worked?
51 According to their T-shirts, who is Tool and who is Guys from the Tool Guys?
52 *Outrageous Fortune* episode titles are all from which Shakespearean play?
53 Name the co-producer of *Outrageous Fortune*.
54 Where do the Wests go camping at Christmas?
55 If Grandpa is dropping the kids off in the pool, where is he headed?
56 Aurora was killed when the motorbike she was riding collided with what vehicle?
57 Which song was playing when Eric seduced Cheryl's sister?
58 Before Loretta took over the Video Hut, what was the nickname she gave to the owner?
59 Which park did Sparky take Baby Jane to?
60 How many children does Corinna Balani have now?

Question 48

Question 59

61 Jethro defended Munter and he was acquitted of stealing what?
62 What is the name of Kasey's brilliant underwear design for men?
63 In which country did Bruce propose to Pascalle?
64 Nicky and Sheree hail from which New Zealand town?
65 Pascalle slept with her half-brother. What was his name?
66 Who is the half-brother's mother and how is she known to the Wests?
67 Wolf worked for a flooring company in Whakatane that was named after a character in *Shortland Street*. What was the company name?
68 What was the character's name on *Shortland Street*?
69 How could this possibly have any relationship to *Outrageous Fortune*?
70 Name four people Jethro slept with while pretending to be Van.

71 Who was Loretta and Pascalle's Irish dancing teacher?
72 When John Leigh appeared on *Shortland Street*, which character did he play?
73 Who does John Leigh play in *Outrageous Fortune*?
74 Is there a bath in the West house bathroom?
75 Which New Zealand children's television presenter did Van have a crush on?
76 What is the name of the rest home owned by Hayden Peters (where Grandpa resided and Pascalle also worked)?
77 Name the rest home resident who beat Derek with his walking stick and was in love with Pascalle.
78 What was the name of Grandpa's regular who Kasey hired for Van?
79 Candy, the Inland Revenue Department lady in Series 4, was played by which actress?
80 What is her family connection to another cast member?
81 What is the name of the beer usually drunk by punters in the Rusty Nail?
82 Name another brand featured on the show.
83 What's Kasey's speciality in the kitchen?
84 Name three guest cast members who also appeared in the television show *Mercy Peak*. (1 point for each)
85 Which two *Outrageous Fortune* actors were the leads in television comedy *Serial Killers*? (1 point for each)

Question 79

86 What is Van's biggest phobia and why?
87 Which member of the West family did Kasey try setting Rochelle up with?
88 What was the name of Pascalle's soft toy that Van set on fire?
89 How old was Rochelle when she lost her virginity?
90 Who did she lose her virginity to?
91 Where did this happen?
92 What is the name of the DoC ranger at the place the Wests go camping at Christmas?
93 One of many West associates is Mule Berenson. Name another member of the Berenson family.
94 Van and Munter are doing up a car. What type is it?
95 What is Van and Munter's dream holiday destination?
96 What is the name of Hayden's bossy eldest sister?
97 Who is the actress who plays her?
98 In real life she has three children with which other cast member?
99 Who is in the middle of the Bahama Triangle?
100 In real life, Robyn Malcolm has two children. What are their names? (1 point for each)

Question 87

(Answers on page 79.)

The official Outrageous Fortune drinking game

The West family likes a drink or two or three or four, from time to time or on a daily basis, and here is the chance to drink with them. **The Official Outrageous Fortune Drinking Game** is designed as an interactive audience-participation cross-platform element, enabling increased enhancement of the viewing experience.

This is not to say that **The Official Outrageous Fortune Drinking Game** and its makers in any way seek to advocate the irresponsible use of alcohol, nor do they condone the consumption of alcohol by minors. You may participate in **The Official Outrageous Fortune Drinking Game** while drinking non-alcoholic beverages such as, say, iced tea or chocolate milk. It will only be half the fun and you will be teased mercilessly, but that is entirely over to you.

(Also please do not play **The Official Outrageous Fortune Drinking Game** while watching Outrageous Fortune on your own as that would be kind of sad.)

(Also do not attempt to play it while watching CSI: Miami or the Jaquie Brown Diaries or any other television show that is not Outrageous Fortune as it will not make any sense.)

How to play

1. Turn on the television and set it to the right channel for *Outrageous Fortune*.
2. Get yourself and your guests something to drink and something to drink out of.
3. Pour yourself and your guests a drink.
4. Wait for *Outrageous Fortune* to start, then follow the simple instructions below until you:
   (a) pass out;
   (b) throw up;
   (c) cannot stand the taste of chocolate milk any more;
   (d) realise *Outrageous Fortune* has finished playing on the telly; and/or
   (e) you run out of things to drink.
5. There are no winners or losers in this game, just drinking. Any dispute about the rules will be sorted out by everybody drinking.

Take ONE SIP of your drink if

- Someone says 'fuck' or any variation;
- Van and/or Munter light up a joint;
- anyone mentions the word 'family';
- Kasey burst into tears;
- Judd uses the phrase 'old man' in relation to Grandpa;
- Grandpa refers to his latest bowel movement;
- there is an excessive display of cleavage;

- Pascalle uses any of the following phrases: 'shooty shoot'; 'huss'; or 'huckery';
- someone wears their sunglasses inside for an unreasonably long time;
- Baby Jane does something extraordinarily cute;
- Falani mentions Mrs Falani;
- a family member gives another family member the traditional West family one-finger salute.

Take a HEARTY MOUTHFUL of your drink if

- There is shagging;
- Cheryl picks up her car keys and/or bag and makes purposefully for the door;
- Van and/or Munter use a pet-name for their penises, for example, 'The Mighty Munt' or 'The Van-an-ator';
- Rochelle announces she's 'in for the long haul' and starts drinking;
- Judd looks long-suffering as a result of something a member of the West family has done;
- Cheryl serves fish pie for dinner;
- any character looks at Loretta, horrified, and says something along the lines of, 'How could you?';

- a vehicle driven by a West family member or associate knocks over something or crashes into another vehicle or generally drives in an irresponsible fashion;
- Jethro gets called a 'Mummy's boy';
- Grandpa talks about his sex life with Ngaire.

DRAIN YOUR GLASS to the very bottom if
- The police raid the house while anyone is having sex;
- Wolf turns up unannounced;
- any of the West family or associates shows their naked bum;
- Grandpa urinates on somebody;
- Pascalle cooks something;
- Loretta tells someone she loves them;
- Eric turns up unannounced;
- Mrs Falani turns up unannounced.

EMPTY THE HOUSE of all alcohol if
- Aurora comes back from the dead.

Acting up — interviews with the cast

Robyn Malcolm

How did you initially prepare for the role you play on Outrageous Fortune?
I spent a great deal of time discussing the world of the show and improvising around that; who these people were, what drives them, what is important to them. Lots of hair, wardrobe and make-up tests. Danced to Guns N' Roses.

What aspect of your character do you like the most?
Her courage. Her direct will. Her lack of need to be liked by people just for the sake of it.

What aspect of your character do you dislike the most?
I don't.

What has been one of the funniest moments you have experienced while filming the show?
When I peed my pants being lifted in the air by bouncers in a strip club in episode 2.

How has playing a high-profile character changed your private and working life?
It's changed it a great deal. I mean I had a sense of that with *Shortland Street*, but this is much more marked. On one hand, it's lovely because people love the show. It's great to be congratulated daily for the job you do — it's a luxury not many people get and enjoy. On the other hand, it makes you a little paranoid. You become used to the fact that in an absent moment when you pick your nose, someone's probably taking a photo on their iPhone!

We understand that an actor's routine while shooting can be quite rigid. Do you use any particular strategies (for example when learning and remembering lines) to help you prepare for what sounds like a very focused and full-on routine while filming?
It depends on the scene really and how my day is going. The strategies vary enormously.

How do you manage to stay in character from series to series?
Easy. The scripts are so character-driven and I know her so well now. It's like putting on your favourite pair of stiletto boots!

Robyn Malcolm

Why do you think Outrageous Fortune *has been so popular?*
Kiwis have fallen in love with themselves through *Outrageous Fortune*. It's about family and how you love and what's important. It hits perfectly the New Zealand sense of humour and pathos. The darker it is, the funnier it is.

Are you actually a cigarette smoker? How do you manage it for the show if you aren't?
I smoked heavily for years. Gave up in 2000. These are herbal cigarettes and they are awful. I found it easy because they bore no resemblance to a real fag.

Because the show has been able to air real domestic issues, do you think it has been able to change social attitudes?
No. I don't think that's the point of this show. It reflects and presents life in a particular way but I don't for a minute subscribe to the notion that it's issues based. We are too un-PC for that.

Grant Bowler

How did you initially prepare for the role you play on Outrageous Fortune*?*
I didn't really need to do too much research. I grew up in Mt Gravatt in Brisbane, which is as close to West Auckland as you can possibly get. There are 500 suburbs in Queensland and Mt Gravatt was voted 498; you should've seen the two suburbs who were voted the worst — they were real shitholes! I grew up in an area where, if you didn't wear the exact uniform of white Dunlop volleys, black cords and a black AC/DC T-shirt with a cloth belt, you got in to a fight on the way to the bus. You either wore the uniform or you fought, one or the other. It was the Angels and AC/DC and later Guns N' Roses and bands like that, Jimmy Barnes, Cold Chisel. I grew up with a mullet and then a mohawk, so preparing for Wolf was going home.

As a kid, I remember these guys who lived down the street; one had an A9X Torana, designed for racing at Bathurst. His buddy had an XU1 Escort. They were the local heroes. We used to go over there every afternoon, and we'd all kind of stand around these cars. Nobody ever started one. We'd just stand around and look at them for hours. So, [to find Wolf] I just kind of went back. I remembered what those guys were like; they were lanky and lean and they were tall and long and they had no bullshit about them and they'd fight you as soon as they met you. But they were really good guys and they took you under their wing and they got to know you.

What was beautiful about the rehearsal process at the beginning of *Outrageous Fortune* was we work-shopped what it is to be working class. You don't smile as much because smiling says 'like me'. You tend to be a lot more direct, a lot more minimalist with what you do, a lot more emotionally and psychologically direct. There's not the level of introspection or naval gazing. Most of the research was internal. I knew how the externals looked because I grew up with it.

What aspect of your character do you like the most?
He's amazingly honest and amazingly courageous. He's an incredibly brave man. Also, he loves for life and he loves with his entire heart. He loves his children no matter what they do to him. He'd die for

each and every member of his family in a millisecond … that's something we trot out but I don't think most people really truly have it in them. He comes at you front on, which personally I really admire.

What aspect of your character do you dislike the most?
I guess his intractability, his inflexibility. You would hope that age would mellow him a bit and that he would learn to bend in the middle, just before breaking, just long enough to get a grip on a situation and know what's going on. He's too reactive. Having said that, people ask me all the time, 'How do you feel playing a bad guy like Wolf?', and I don't think he's done anything in this show that I find irredeemable. I find all of it understandable and well within the scope of human action. I think some of the things he does, for instance when he screamed at Loretta or when he nearly whacked her one once, I think they're things we hide in our own living rooms and we never admit happen, but I'll bet you 99.9999% of parents have felt that.

What has been one of the funniest moments you have experienced while filming the show?
Funniest moment on-screen for Wolf is still the Eric/Wolf rock scene with the rock with Eric's ankle bracelet. It was actually one of the most wonderful moments in my career because Brian Sergent completely directed that scene. Simon Bennett [the director] and I took a backseat and Brian told us the timings, what should happen when and he was absolutely right — it was perfect.
Funniest off-screen moment; God, there are so many! So many days of just crying with laughter I can't pin one down, but *Outrageous Fortune* is always a joy. I guess on some days the sheer level of inappropriate sexual contact with members of the crew (MALE members of the crew … because you wouldn't want to do anything wrong by the girls).

We understand that an actor's routine while shooting can be quite rigid. Do you use any particular strategies (for example when learning and remembering lines) to help you prepare for what sounds like a very focused and full-on routine while filming?
What I do is I make sure I get plenty of sleep and then, if I'm shooting stuff that's highly emotional, sometimes I won't speak to people much at all, other than one word answers all day. And crew get on to that really, really quickly. At first I think people think you're really angry or something but it's not that. It's that, if I come out and be nice to you when I've got to become enraged in a scene, I'm actually breaking my focus and I'm not doing what I'm paid to do. So I go still, I go really, really quiet and I go into myself and I rest. Every moment I'm not working, I'm resting. I don't expend energy on social niceties.

If I've got to do something where I've got to crack myself open and become vulnerable, I know that my body finds that hard to hold relentlessly all day, so I might go through patches, like waves, an hour or two hours at a time. I can feel it now because I've been doing it for 20 years, so when the wave starts to pass and when I start to come out of that emotion (whether it be grief or pain or sorrow), I'll come back out and joke around for a while and lighten myself up, and then I'll get still again and wait for the next wave. As an artist, and I don't know how it is for everybody else, these things tend to come in waves and it's a matter of timing it so that I can catch the wave at the right moment, which is when the camera rolls.

Grant Bowler

If I've got to do anything that requires an enormous amount of confidence and bravado or arrogance, I normally spend the entire day horsing around, cracking jokes and generally kind of entreating myself with the crew because the more at home and the more confident I feel, the better. Acting is a confidence trick, it really is.

How do you manage to stay in character from series to series?
Put on the boots! I've been playing him so long and I know him so well that's it's literally that. I remember coming back for the second season. I got a bit nervous, very nervous actually. And then the third season, because I came in right at the end I'd been away for a year and a half which is a long time, I got nervous then. But when I came back for series four I knew exactly where I was from the first moment. Four was an interesting exercise for me because I knew the character arc for the series so what I decided to do was to push every single member of the viewing public away from Wolf so they all hated him for the first eight episodes, and then win them back in episodes nine and ten. It was like an acting experiment for myself; I just let him off the leash for eight episodes and then spent two episodes cracking him open and bringing him back — and it worked so that was good!

Why do you think Outrageous Fortune *has been so popular?*
Because by and large it speaks the truth. It gets rid of a lot of the niceties of people, it deconstructs a lot of family dynamics and lets us explore them in a more honest, raw and real way. Everybody's a battler, everybody's well-intentioned and also, they lose. Most TV shows you watch the characters don't really risk anything and they've got an enormous amount to lose. These people risk an enormous amount and they've got bugger all. And I think most of the audience can identify with that. My one desire for *Outrageous Fortune* is that it never moves into a realm that's too civilised, where we start arguing ideas rather than the visceral. There's gotta be blood and jail at the end of it otherwise we're talking abstracts and there's too much television that talks about that.

Antony Starr

What aspect of your characters do you like the most?
I like the complexity of Jethro and the simplicity of Van.

What aspect of your characters do you dislike the most?
The simplicity of Van and the complexity of Jethro. Actually I really like them both and I don't judge them.

What has been one of the funniest moments you have experienced while filming the show?
Any scene with Dave Fane (Falani) or Brian Sergent (Eric). They are hilarious.

How has playing such high-profile characters changed your private and working life?
There has been a fantastic public response to the show. It's great to be involved with a show that is so well loved. It's been a great ride.

Antony Starr

We understand that an actor's routine while shooting can be quite rigid. Do you use any particular strategies (for example when learning and remembering lines) to help you prepare for what sounds like a very focused and full-on routine while filming?
I have no specific routines because the shoot is constantly changing. I think it would vary from actor to actor.

How do you manage to stay in character from series to series?
I put myself in Cryo-Freeze in the off-time.

Why do you think Outrageous Fortune *has been so popular?*
I think it's probably because it's so well produced. Also the characters are down to earth and real. Kiwis seem to like that.

Is that real dope you smoke on the programme?
Yes. We are high all day long.

Other than the obvious differences in intelligence, is there a mantra or set of character foibles you use or have created to help you clearly distinguish between Van and Jethro?
No. The characters are quite familiar to me now. Possibly Van is looser, Jethro more rigid.

How do wardrobe and make-up make a difference in helping you keep the twins as clear and separate characters?
They have a huge impact. Particularly in the beginning when we were creating the characters. We were spoilt with the calibre of the crew making the show. They are amazing.

Siobhan Marshall

How did you initially prepare for the role you play on Outrageous Fortune?
When I auditioned for *Outrageous Fortune* I was in the South Island filming *The Lion, the Witch and the Wardrobe*, so my fellow female centaurs and I did lots of fake modelling and Carmen Electra-style strip dancing to get me ready. Obviously in series 1, Pascalle's main aspiration is to be a model and she does some pretty risqué things! I also got a spray tan for my audition, which I feel a bit bad about now because I kind of tricked them into thinking I was all golden brown. I am pale.

What aspect of your character do you like the most?
Pascalle is overall an honest human being. She doesn't really play too many games. What you see is what you get — I respect that.

What aspect of your character do you dislike the most?
After all these years playing Pascalle, the only thing I can really think of is her ditzy-ness. Sometimes I love it, other times I get embarrassed when I read some of her lines. I have to remind myself, 'It's not me, it's not me.'

What has been one of the funniest moments you have experienced while filming the show?
Hmmm, we have good giggles quite often on set. The time we were filming Antonia (Loretta) doing her Irish dancing was quite a good one. She was dancing intensely, angry and very focused and the next minute both her chicken fillet boobs fell out (Loretta was pregnant at the time). It was hilarious!

How has playing such a high-profile character changed your private and working life?
Privately it hasn't really changed. With my working life, it has given me a fabulous job and an excellent experience.

We understand that an actor's routine while shooting can be quite rigid. Do you use any particular strategies (for example when learning and remembering lines) to help you prepare for what sounds like a very focused and full-on routine while filming?
Not really. The lines are pretty easy to learn. I think good writing is easy to learn because it is natural to say and it makes complete sense.
I make sure I get enough sleep — that is a big one for me. If I'm a bit tired I don't give it the same energy I do when I'm not. If I have an emotional or tiring scene, I always try to sleep before it.

How do you manage to stay in character from series to series?
It's through the writing mainly and having good directors.

Siobhan Marshall

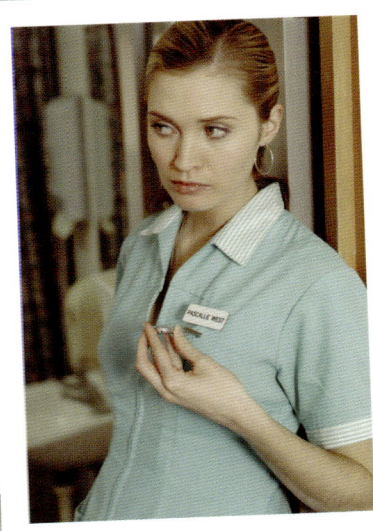

Why do you think Outrageous Fortune *has been so popular?*
Because everyone can relate to some aspect of it. I have people come up to me and tell me about their daughter or friend being just like Pascalle, Loretta or another character on the show.

Is there a real person on whom you modelled your character?
Yes! But I can't say who.

Are you as much a follower of fashion as your character?
No, I'm definitely a creature of comfort. I like nice clothes but I don't really keep up with fashion. I like what I like.

Antonia Prebble

How did you initially prepare for the role you play on Outrageous Fortune?
I moved to West Auckland! I'm from Wellington so I auditioned for the part down there. I had to move up to Auckland before we started filming, obviously, and a friend had a spare room in her flat in New Lynn, so I thought, what better way to get into character than become a Westie myself. So I did that, and also, on the advice of the producer, I spent quite a bit of time at the PAK'nSAVE in Henderson, which gives you invaluable insights into Westie culture.

What aspect of your character do you like the most?
I like that she's really intelligent because it means she has huge scope in terms of the types of things she can realistically be involved with, so her storylines are always really interesting to play.

What aspect of your character do you dislike the most?
Speaking subjectively, as the actor that plays her, there's nothing I dislike about her, but objectively, if I were to meet her on the street, I think I'd dislike the fact that she's very self-focused.

What has been one of the funniest moments you have experienced while filming the show?
This is a hard question to answer as there have been so many funny times, but one that stands out is filming the scene where Pascalle is hosting a dinner party for Bruce Khan's supposedly Muslim sister, Linda. It was only the female characters in the scene, and so all of us just turned into silly, squawking women! We were in the mood where everything and everyone was absolutely hilarious, so we were in hysterics the whole time. The poor director was trying his best to keep us in line but we just couldn't help ourselves, a few actors actually had to be sent off set because they couldn't hold it together. I have to say that when I watched that episode, I didn't find the scene nearly as funny as when we filmed it, I guess it was just one of those 'you had to be there' moments.

How has playing such a high-profile character changed your private and working life?
Not as much as you might think. I get recognised when I go out now, but New Zealanders are pretty laid back, so the recognition is never too intrusive. Professionally speaking, not a lot has changed either; I haven't had any big-time producers knocking down my door because they've seen *Outrageous* or anything. In many ways, doing a high-profile show like this can actually limit your opportunities to

Antonia Prebble

work in other shows because people find it difficult to disassociate you from such a familiar character. I'm crossing my fingers that won't happen to me; only time will tell!

We understand that an actor's routine while shooting can be quite rigid. Do you use any particular strategies (for example when learning and remembering lines) to help you prepare for what sounds like a very focused and full-on routine while filming?

It is pretty rigid but because it is an ensemble show, we do all get time off so the schedule is totally manageable. With regard to scene preparation and line learning, I make sure I'm really familiar with the content of the scene at least a few days in advance of filming it (or more time if it's an important scene), but I generally leave learning the lines to the night before as I find that's the best way to keep them at the top of my brain.

How do you manage to stay in character from series to series?

We've been doing it for so long it almost feels like second nature now; I just sort of slip into Loretta mode as soon as I put on my costume. But I think the main reason that it is so easy to do that is because the writing is so good. As soon as I read a new script I can hear Loretta's voice in my head, and everything else just flows on from there.

Why do you think Outrageous Fortune *has been so popular?*

Fundamentally, I think it's because the quality of the writing is exceptional. It's funny and heart-breaking at the same time, often in the same scene even. All the characters are likable and relatable and no one's trying to be cool.

I think New Zealanders take exception to people who are pretentious or trying to fit themselves into an international mould. The Wests are 'warts-and-all' kind of people. They are who they are and make no apologies for it, and I think that kind of honesty is a quality people find endearing.

We understand you originally auditioned for the character of Pascalle but you were eventually cast as Loretta. Why do you think you were considered better suited for the character of Loretta?

Good question. I do feel like I'm pretty different to Loretta in many ways, but, at the same time, from my first audition I felt I implicitly understood her, she sat really easily in me; I knew how she talked, how she carried herself and why she feels the way she does about the world. Loretta approaches everything from an intellectual point of view, and I think I also have a tendency to do that, whereas Pascalle always acts according to her instincts. I think that is quite a significant distinction in terms of why certain actors are better suited to different roles.

Frank Whitten

How did you initially prepare for the role you play on Outrageous Fortune?
I was cast. I read the first script. I turned up for work. The rest is my little secret.

What aspect of your character do you like the most? What aspect of your character do you dislike the most?
I don't think of my characters in those terms. That way … lies — and also bad acting.

What has been one of the funniest moments you have experienced while filming the show?
When my prosthetic penis refused to stop piddling long after a take was completed. A great deal of diluted apple juice was sacrificed in the cause of low comedy on that day. I have named the offending article Eric, after the children's book *Eric, or Little by Little*.

How has playing such a high profile character changed your private and working life?
As my private life is private, I can't comment. As for work, it does and will affect my chances of playing other roles, particularly in television. But not, hopefully, my ability to do theatre in Australia where the wages are good enough for it not to be a charitable act — which, alas, seems to be true in New Zealand.
To be positive, however, people seem to be more interested in what I have in my supermarket trolley (which has cured my shoplifting tendencies). And instead of being thrown out of night clubs, I'm requested now (politely) to vacate the premises in my own time. On all fours if needs must.

We understand that an actor's routine while shooting can be quite rigid. Do you use any particular strategies (for example when learning and remembering lines) to help you prepare for what sounds like a very focused and full-on routine while filming?
I don't have a life.

How do you manage to stay in character from series to series?
The real problem is how to stay out of it during the breaks.

Why do you think Outrageous Fortune has been so popular?
Because television was invented.

You play the character of an endearing, somewhat bumbling because of age, well-respected safecracker and horny older gentleman. Is there anyone on whom you model your character?
The character is the writers' creation more than he is mine. My modest constitution knows no source other than my imagination. And why would I confess to basing him on a real person anyway? They'd sue the pants off me, stupid.

Are you at all like Grandpa?
No. So fuck off! (Whoops!)

Playing the part

Behind the scenes...

Episode summaries

SERIES 1

Episode 1   *Slings and Arrows*
When career criminal Wolfgang West gets put away for four years, his wife Cheryl decides it's time for her family to go straight. Although son Jethro is the first West ever to graduate university (as a lawyer), it's a tough ask for a family where his identical twin Van is being sought in conjunction with a home invasion on a wealthy Asian businessman, daughter Pascalle has been posing for dodgy pictures to further her modelling career, and youngest Loretta is a recidivist wagger. Oh, and Grandpa has moved in after burning down his unit. But Cheryl's had enough; they're getting out of the crime game. The general consensus, from everyone from Wolf to the family's nemesis, Detective Sergeant Wayne Judd, is that this can't be done.

Episode 2   *The Rub*
Cheryl's plan to march her family down the straight and narrow road has not got off to a good start; and there's only so much mince a family can eat by candlelight after the power's cut off before tempers begin to fray. Working as a pool-boy and driver for the Hong family, Van finds himself the object of Mrs Hong's affections. Pascalle's modelling career is under severe threat, but while working at the Snapper Shack fish'n'chip shop, she gets discovered! Meanwhile, Cheryl's new job as a supermarket checkout chick teaches her that being on the right side of the law doesn't necessarily mean being honest, especially when Wolf is in the mix.

Episode 3   *A Little More Than Kin*
Jethro's supposed Maori heritage comes under fire when a lawyerly 'colleague' starts to question the West family whakapapa. Jethro thinks his colleague is after his job, but finds he wants his body. Cheryl receives unwanted attention from two of Wolf's best mates, leaving Wolf imagining the worst. Wolf's jealousy leads him to dob one of them in, leaving Cheryl jobless yet again. Cheryl realises Wolf's role and tells him she doesn't want to see him for a while. Wolf is defiant to the end — he'll be right there when she does.

Episode 4   *The Cause of this Defect*
It's Billy (The Kid) Grady West's funeral. He may have been Eric's son, but the Wests were his true family. Granted leave from prison to attend the funeral, Wolf makes a triumphant return. Triumphant for everyone but Cheryl, that is. While the wake is in full swing, Loretta sees the opportunity to no longer be the oldest virgin in West Auckland and seduces her dad's prison guard. She's underwhelmed by her first experience of sex. When Cheryl observes Wolf in action with his family and friends, she realises Wolf is still pulling the strings and can never change. If she wants her family to survive, she can't be with him any more. So the best thing that can possibly happen is that Wolf stays in prison for as long as possible.

Episode 5   *The Infants of Spring*
Cheryl has sunk to an all-time low. Even her offspring are worried about her, so spurred on by Jethro's example of how to be a loving son, they each resolve to do their bit to help out. Pascalle's big break leads her to be persuaded to try stripping, as Wolf sets Van up on a job with Sparky, electrician by trade, arsonist by calling. Jethro helps Van out so that he can be in two places at once and roots Tracy Hong while disguised as Van. Meanwhile Mrs Hong announces her pregnancy — is Van the baby's daddy? Loretta saves the Video Hut and in this way, scores her dream job as manager of her own business.

Episode 6   *But Never Doubt I Love*
Grandpa is not in a good headspace and Loretta is assigned to look after him but she manages to lose him. Grandpa is found happy at the home of Margaret who, it transpires, used to be Mark, Grandpa's former partner in crime and prison cellmate. Loretta is not impressed with the liaison. Constable Hickey's infatuation with Pascalle leads Judd to help Cheryl, but at the same time blows Pascalle's job as a stripper. Meanwhile, Loretta discovers that Grandpa's trannie love is also a cover for a big job.

Episode 7 Foul Deeds Will Rise
A big day approaches for the West clan. Well, for Cheryl and Jethro — the rest of the family are going to join in whether they want to or not. It's Jethro's admission to the Bar, his final hurdle in becoming a fully-fledged lawyer. Jethro and Caroline decide to 'out' themselves as a couple at the admission ceremony. Grandpa announces that he and Margaret are moving away together — but not before one last job. Loretta's life of truancy and manipulation starts to unravel and when blackmail fails, Loretta faces the true horror of school. But she forces Margaret to leave town and breaks Grandpa's heart.

Episode 8 My Dearest Foe
It's Cheryl's birthday. Her present from the kids is an ugly cuckoo clock, which is the first of many things that spoil her day; her family is less than supportive about her new job at an insurance company; her car breaks down on the way to work; and her friend Kasey files a dodgy insurance claim. Pascalle battles to win a modelling job for an animal charity but she's up against Chantelle 'Garbage Guts' Lazenby, a former fat-girl from Irish dancing who is now a complete hottie. The *Top Model*-style catfight escalates, until Pascalle loses the job but her final act of revenge is to 'donate' all of Chantelle's clothing to a charity-recycling bin. It's all about charity, isn't it? At home, Grandpa uses Munter's sympathy over the loss of Margaret to lure him into a game of poker. It is a game that will go on for several days, as Grandpa fleeces Munter, Eric and Rochelle of their money; which makes Grandpa feel a lot better.

Episode 9 When the Blood Burns
Van moves from being the Hong's lap dog to managing Mr Hong's bargain basement shop, the Lucky Dollar store. His first day as manager turns into a disaster when he believes the Doslic family's courier company have been misappropriating Lucky Dollar stock. When Mr Hong cancels the courier contract, it transpires that Van has inadvertently sparked a race war between West Auckland's Chinese and Dalmatian communities. The twins are divided; Jethro launches an affair with Tracy while Draska comes to more than Van's defence. Eric gets beaten up as the sacrificial lamb, without ever quite understanding why he's getting the shit kicked out of him by the West Auckland United Nations.

Episode 10 The Fat Weed That Roots Itself
Pascalle finds her Rod, in the form of television personality Grant Wilkes and gets papparazzied. But when Grant's wife appears on the scene, all is not what Pascalle dreamed. Cheryl's burgeoning lingerie business Hoochie Mama takes a massive order from the female cops of West Auckland, but when Kasey lends the deposit to her dodgy boyfriend Murray for a P-deal, Cheryl takes it upon herself to track the money down. While on the case, Cheryl walks straight into the middle of a drug bust, but she's saved by DS Judd. Something of a bond is built between the two of them.

Episode 11 It Cannot Come to Good
Pascalle calls time on her fifteen minutes of fame when she dumps Grant, but he doesn't take the news well. Van's visit to Wolf leaves him bound to help his father's case. He comes up with the Tongan job and enlists Munter to help. They make off with the cash, but realise they've been caught on tape. As the boys start to panic, Draska leaps into action and takes control. She disappears with Munter and the money, leaving Van to destroy the video evidence. When she resurfaces, she has a plan to explain how they got the money: it was given to them by her relatives — so they can pay for Van and Draska's wedding, of course. And, in this way, Van gets engaged. Having been labelled a nark, Cheryl's forced to take refuge in a motel. Judd follows and she invites him in for a drink and one thing leads to another … they end up in bed together: the final consummation of an affair that's been building since that knock on the door on the day that Wolf was put away.

Episode 12 To Be Honest as this World Goes
Someone is paying Corky, the West family's dodgy P-smoking lawyer, to go ahead with Wolf's appeal — but Cheryl has no idea who the mysterious benefactor is. For her, the pending appeal raises the spectre of Wolf getting out of prison — just as she has embarked on an affair with Judd. Jethro's discovery that Judd has planted evidence causes him to switch sides and defend his father, perhaps for the first time ever. Cheryl finds out about the Tongan job and sees Van as having betrayed everything she's tried to do for her family — so Van and Draska are no longer welcome in the family home.

Episode 13 Go, Bid the Soldiers Shoot
Wolf and Jethro's plans to free Wolf (and nail Judd for his creative use of evidence) are proceeding at pace. Cheryl delivers an ultimatum to Wolf: if he uses the evidence against Judd in his appeal, then Van will go to jail — and if Van goes to jail, then Cheryl won't be waiting for Wolf when he gets out. She will leave him if he sacrifices his son. Each of the Wests, in their individual way, takes their revenge on Draska. So despite the fact that Van and Draska don't end up married, the series ends with a West party: Wolf's on home detention; Judd and Cheryl are parted; Van is a free man; Pascalle is in the sack with Kurt; Loretta is despairing of her family … In other words, everything is just where it should be.

Episode summaries

SERIES 2

Episode 1   *Thy Name is Woman*
Early morning roots at the West house are interrupted when Judd arrives to make an arrest. This time it's Loretta who is in trouble with the law. Down at the station, Loretta learns her Video Hut employee Kurt has been talking to the cops. Wolf is certain that Loretta's arrest is Judd's attempt to get at him. Wolf confronts Loretta; crime is the domain of men. Stay out of it. Van is in trouble over the missing money from the Tongan job, but as Loretta plans to flee with her ill-gotten gains, Wolf gets his hands on it. To Cheryl's chagrin, Wolf consolidates his position as he squares things up with the Tongans and affects The Great Reconciliation between the Wests and the Doslics. Grievances are vented to everyone's satisfaction until Draska drops the bomb — she's pregnant.

Episode 2   *Think Yourself a Baby*
Hoochie Mama, despite raging parties, is not a raging success. An unlikely saviour steps up to the plate: Mrs Doslic wants to invest in the company. Cheryl isn't so keen and tries to secure a legitimate bank loan. Wolf kiboshes this by flaunting his home detention ankle bracelet. But when Jethro shows Tracy some of Hoochie's wares, Cheryl has herself an investor. She's not so pleased about Van facing forced parenthood with Draska, but Munter discovers Draska has used a pregnant Corrina Balani's pee to pass Cheryl's pregnancy test. So Draska is again ousted. Meanwhile, Pascalle's helping out at the Video Hut where she meets Hayden Peters. Pascalle reckons he's the perfect man, except … he doesn't seem to be interested in her. But once Hayden realises Pascalle's family connections, it's all on.

Episode 3   *The Secrets of My Prison House*
Pascalle's new man Hayden seeks Wolf's approval and gets him a job and out of the house. But he has an ulterior motive that Wolf's parole officer would not approve of … Jethro has quit his job at the firm and set up on his own in Corky's old office. Grandpa and Loretta show a keen interest in his new premises and Grandpa teaches Loretta all there is to know about safecracking.

Episode 4   *This Two-Fold Force*
Loretta's 16th birthday approaches — and in the West family this is a big event (you might be in prison or dead before your 21st). For Loretta, turning 16 means she can leave school. But to her shock, her warring parents are for once united in their opposition and enrol her in a Catholic school. But Loretta bests them by engaging the help of a wayward teen, Jools, to be her school doppelganger. Meanwhile Van and Munter are on a big job — a truck full of crayfish — what a score. Van proudly offers to cut his dad in, but when Eric provides dodgy freezers, the deal and the crays are off.

Episode 5   *Shall We To the Court?*
Wolf has a case for Jethro: Sparky is currently in the cells on a serious arson charge — and Jethro will get him off. At Wolf's suggestion, Van reluctantly agrees to take the stand as the key witness to Sparky's whereabouts on the night in question, but nerves kick in. Munter suggests his mum's special cookies might help Van relax. Which they do — a little too much. Jethro realises his brother is stoned — at which point an obvious (but highly risky) plan occurs — and they swap identities. Jethro's plan works, but leaves Judd suspicious. Pascalle fantasises about Hayden's marital intentions; Hoochie Mama fantasy gets a man literally crotchless but Tracy saves the day.

Episode 6   *The Affliction of His Love*
At the Rusty Nail, the first Hoochie Girl competition is underway. Van is surprised to see his first love, Aurora Bay, on the runway. But after the show Aurora flees, Cinderella-like, leaving behind only a g-string. As Van pines for his long-lost love, Pascalle reveals Aurora is now a living with a gang, the Horsemen, and has hooked up with the gang's leader, Tyson. Van is determined to rescue his princess. At a hotel rendezvous, Judd suggests to a fuming Cheryl that she leaves Wolf. But Cheryl can't do this without losing her family — and she's not prepared for that. When Judd leaves the next day he doesn't notice Jethro. Unaccustomed as she is to having feelings, Loretta displays strange symptoms, until Grandpa enlightens her: she's got the hots for Hayden.

Episode 7   *All That Fortune, Death and Danger Dare*
Cheryl is sympathetic when she hears about Van's wish to save Aurora. But Van cracks and tells his mum about the big job: a major drug deal is being planned by several biker gangs and Wolf is planning to steal the cash. Needless to say, Cheryl is furious with Wolf. Judd arrives at the Rusty Nail to see Cheryl. She wants Wolf stopped and out of the picture, before it's too late — whatever it takes. Wolf's phone rings. It's Judd. He just had a drink with Cheryl. It was very convivial. Though not half as much fun as when he was in bed with her. Wolf storms in to the Rusty Nail only to find that Judd is with Hickey and a number of off-duty police officers. He has violated his parole. Wolf whacks Judd before escaping. Cheryl arrives home to find a bloody hacksaw and Wolf's home detention ankle bracelet, which has been hacked off. Cheryl looks at the sawn-off band. It's the end of her marriage. But where is Wolf?

Episode 8 *The Steep and Thorny Way to Heaven*
Van hatches a plan and enlists Munter's help to free Aurora from the clutches of the Horsemen. Jethro tells Van that Cheryl's getting it on with Judd. However, Van backs Judd because he understands what it's like to be in love with a woman he can't have. As Cheryl gets drunk with her daughters and confesses her affair with Judd, the job at the gang headquarters gets under way. Sparky's love affair with the flame throws the job into confusion, but Wolf ensures that the money is safe. Judd lets Wolf get away, but later arrives at the West house. A car has been found in the bush, burnt out. There were possessions that belonged to Wolf in it. Cheryl and her daughters take in the news.

Episode 9 *To Be, Or Not To Be*
Pascalle takes it upon herself to hunt for the missing Wolf and enlists the help of Munter and Eric. Cheryl visits Judd on his home turf for the first time and discovers a shrine to hunting; is it possible that Wolf was his prey? Judd explains it all away and he knows she's been feeling conflicted. But Cheryl's not feeling that conflicted right now, and as proof she kisses him. Van and Aurora are ready to disappear, when Tyson storms into the house. Aurora steps forward and tells Tyson that she loves Van. He accepts her choice but, just before he leaves as a broken man, he punches Van out.

Episode 10 *The Indifferent Children of the Earth*
Hoochie Mama has expanded and at the opening of their new premises, the Wests are taken by surprise when Judd appears. Back at the West house, Cheryl discovers that while she's been keeping Judd's bed warm, Aurora's been keeping the home fires burning. Elsewhere at the Video Hut, Loretta has been engaged in quelling insurrection in the form of Jools, her stand-in at school. Jools has been making quite a splash on the swim team, making friends, and getting noticed — altogether unacceptable behaviour. And Loretta is not one to take it lying down.

Episode 11 *Get Thee to Bed*
Tracy Hong is kidnapped by none other than Eric. When the Hongs refuse to pay the ransom Tracy takes control and manipulates her own kidnapping. At the Video Hut, life is going well for Loretta — until Hayden enters. He asks her to read a script, which turns out to be porn. Loretta is disgusted. Hayden mounts a challenge: if she hates it that much, try writing a better script. Later when Loretta visits Hayden at home, it's more like a scene from their own porn film as they finally act upon their feelings. Meanwhile, Cheryl leads Judd into the West house. No-one else is there, but he's still nervous — is she sure about this? You bet she is.

Episode 12 *By a Brother's Hand*
Aurora and Van's house-hunting leaves Munter alone and out in the cold. When Van is refused a loan he finds a plan B: Wolf's money that Jethro has stashed away. Van is furious when Jethro refuses to help and later steals Jethro's car. But Jethro gets his revenge by stepping in as Van in order to impregnate Mrs Hong. Tensions between Jethro and Cheryl escalate and Jethro crosses the ultimate line and hits his mother. Tracy witnesses this and leaves Jethro forever. Pascalle's community service at the Janet Frame Rest Home turns into her dream job.

Episode 13 *An Old Man Is Twice a Child*
Grandpa's mental state continues to deteriorate and Cheryl wants to put him in a home. The family is appalled — but no-one's willing to look after him. But Jethro pulls some strings with Hayden. To Grandpa's chagrin, he's moved into the Janet Frame, but he has Pascalle to care for him as well as the doctor she's keen on, Bruce Khan. Back at the house, the rest of the family cleans out Grandpa's caravan and Cheryl discovers Wolf's will — which reveals that he has a second family …

Episode 14 *Fathers, Mothers, Daughters, Sons*
Cheryl announces to the family that they have another brother, Brandon Gibbs. Loretta laughs, Pascalle cries — it transpires Pascalle has slept with Brandon. If you accidentally sleep with your half-brother, can that be counted as incest? Loretta's deal with Jools begins to unravel when Jools' media studies short film *Jandal* has a public screening at the school. The insinuation that a family friend molested Loretta shocks the family, and also shocks Pascalle's new boyfriend, Bruce. Judd decides to leave the police force for Cheryl — and also finds a way to contact Wolf. But does Cheryl want that number?

Episode 15 *O God!*
Wolf is back to visit Grandpa who has had surgery on his brain tumour — but who knows what else Wolf's up to? Sparky has seen the burning light and arrives at the police station and confesses to Judd all his sins and those of some others, including Van and Jethro. Judd tells Cheryl. To keep Sparky from telling the world about a certain robbery, she sends Van and Aurora to babysit the arsonist. Van and Aurora lose Sparky who goes to the Rusty Nail and tells all to Tyson. The next day Cheryl arrives home to an empty house — they've been done over by the Horsemen. She blames Wolf for this entirely. Despite all this, Van proposes to Aurora. When Bruce confesses to Pascalle that he's a virgin, she claims she is too.

Episode 16 *Now Cracks a Noble Heart*
The house is in uproar when fleas are discovered in furniture loaned from Eric. Judd buys new furniture with his perf money. Eric is left wounded — but fortunately he finds a sympathetic ear in Wolf, who wants to hear all the affairs of the West home. Wolf's back and he's got big plans, not just for his kids … Meanwhile, Pascalle is determined to reconstitute her virginity, but reconstructive surgery is expensive. When Hayden offers her a part in the film he's making with Loretta, Pascalle has some misgivings when she learns what sort of film it is, but decides it will be worth it in the end. The morning after Van and Aurora's engagement party, cars converge on the West house and cops arrest Judd who is accused of being paid off by criminals. Cheryl realises that this is Wolf's revenge — and he did it to get back at her.

Xmas Special *Wherein Our Saviour's Birth is Celebrated*
Judd is unable to get bail as the West family head off on their annual holiday pilgrimage to Tutaekuri Bay, a DOC cold water campsite. There Loretta loves to torture the DOC ranger, and everyone has a fun-filled family Christmas. But joining them this time is Jeanette, Cheryl's religious sister who has left her husband and family. And when they arrive at Tutaekuri Bay, the Wests are appalled to find the Doslics are already encamped and in their spot. Americans have also taken over rights to the secret beach round the corner. This is officially War, played out in various acts of petty aggression. Loretta finds that she's met her match in the DOC Ranger, Graeme, and ends up having to guard dotterels and getting it on with Graeme. Munter pips Jethro to the post and ends up with a beautiful American hottie. Pascalle is missing her beloved Bruce, but decides to try and make peace between Jeanette and Cheryl. In this she's not entirely successful, but Jeanette finds consolation with Eric. And Pascalle finds out why her mother is so attached to Tutaekuri Bay. She and Wolf had a baby before the twins — Helena, who died in utero. This is the place where her ashes are scattered. Aurora bests Draska in a final Wests v Doslics challenge, which ends up in a cat fight. Eventually the Wests unite to reclaim the secret beach as Judd finally gets out on bail to join them.

SERIES 3
Episode 1 *What Loss Your Honour May Sustain*
Early morning peace and love at the West House is once again disrupted by a raid. This time, the cops, led by Judd's ex Monica, are on a campaign — looking for a reason for Judd to breach his bail conditions. Cheryl's not one to take police harassment lightly, but when Monica pushes her too far, Judd steps in to defend her — and is arrested. Van discovers that the Lucky Dollar store is being sold — and with it all of Van's dreams of a career and a way to pay for his wedding. His search for the culprit leads him, via Jethro and Jethro's mole in the Council (Treena), to a developer called Gary Savage. Van and Munter steal Gary's earthmoving equipment, and Gary does a deal. Van can start planning his wedding again, with Munter his best man.

Episode 2 *While the Grass Grows*
Cheryl's determination to get Judd out of prison is hampered by Grandpa's determination to keep Judd inside — and out of the family. Loretta's porn film is advancing, but still lacks a leading man. Hayden sees big potential in Munter's equipment, but Munter's confused by Hayden's seemingly gay advances. Meanwhile, as Aurora works two jobs for the wedding, Van's noble gesture to save money on drugs is growing dope in Grandpa's caravan. Van and Munter, paid off by Loretta, have the cash they need to score, only to find the tinny house is run by scary Tyson. But there's worse to come for Van; helping Tyson is none other than Van's princess, Aurora …

Episode 3 *Most True, She is a Strumpet*
Loretta discovers that Grandpa is seeing Hayley the hooker, and doesn't take it well. Meanwhile, Van's discovery that Aurora is involved with her ex, Tyson, causes Van all kinds of mental anguish, compounded by the surprise arrival of Aurora's lesbian biker mum, Pam. Cheryl takes a firm hand with Aurora. She has to choose between Tyson and Van because Van can't take this kind of confusion. Aurora promises Van she will leave Tyson. Van still doesn't trust her and goes to Tyson's house, where he misconstrues her farewells with Tyson. Distraught, he does what a West never does and makes a call … Later, an angry Tyson confronts Van in the pub; Aurora took Tyson's stash of dope to protect him from the cops and as she rode off on a bike, she had an accident. Aurora is dead.

Episode 4 *Contagious Blastments*
As Van struggles with his guilt over Aurora's death, Cheryl tries to make peace with Pam so the Wests can attend Aurora's funeral. Meanwhile, Hayden becomes an unlikely accomplice to a funeral home break-in as Van tries to give Aurora the Viking funeral she wanted. On finding that they've taken the wrong body, Munter confronts Van. Cheryl gets nowhere with Pam, so there's only one thing for it and that's to gear up for a funeral-crashing. Who needs a cricket bat? As the family sets off Van is missing. When Jethro discovers him, he also discovers the truth; that Van dobbed and set in motion the chain of events that caused Aurora's death. Cheryl brings Van home so that they can have a proper send-off for Aurora in the back yard. Tragedy brings people together and there is much rooting; Kasey and Munter, Loretta and Hayden. And Pascalle returns from Pakistan. Van watches a rowboat burn as Grandpa informs him that he is cursed forever. Van is happy to be cursed.

Episode 5 What Did You Enact?
Pascalle's return brings some good news — she's engaged to Bruce. Thankfully for Loretta, Pascalle still needs to be in the porn ('erotica for women') film so she can pay for her hymen reconstruction. As production gets under way, tension rises between the director (Loretta) and the producer (Hayden) and Pascalle fears that Bruce or Cheryl will find out what she's up to. As Bruce seeks Pascalle and Munter walks in on Kasey coaching Pascalle through a lesbian scene, everything seems set for disaster. The comedy of errors ends up with Kasey and Munter back together and Pascalle admitting to Bruce that she's more experienced than she let on. He's happy with that and Pascalle exits the movie. She no longer needs reconstruction.

Episode 6 Put the Strong Law on Him
When Pascalle discovers that Van's room and mind are both something of a hygiene disaster she becomes obsessed by a desire to cleanse. But Van's obsession with Aurora's thong proves something of a barrier. Meanwhile, Cheryl continues her fight for Judd's release and on Gary Savage's advice gets a new lawyer, Des Stewart. Judd is not so cheered at the thought of the huge expense, but Cheryl is determined. Des pursues the personal angle, which to Cheryl's shock reveals that Judd's marriage to Monica ended over an affair, with the wife of a criminal. Jethro feels the pressure from Gary to pursue a case against former West family lawyer Corky and later discovers that Gary's beef against Corky is apparently at Wolf's instruction. Cheryl takes up a loan offer from Gary to cover Judd's legal fees and Judd is released on bail.

Episode 7 I Dare Damnation
Judd's happiness at being home is undermined by being both cashless and having to break down the toilet door to rescue Van, again. When Draska reappears on the scene Van seems hell bent on destruction and disaster. Cheryl is driven to the ultimate threat: expelling Van from the house. At this, Munter decides to take Van to the Coromandel to stay with his mum and clean up. But when Munter's mum, Karla, brings out her infamous cookies and Van steals booze, Munter finds himself in the grip of a full body stone, watching powerlessly as Karla falls off the wagon and Van gets it on with his mum. Munter feels betrayed, but Van is unrepentant. As Munter drives away, the unthinkable has happened — Van and Munter have broken up.

Episode 8 O Horrible, Most Horrible!
Cheryl tries to repair the hole in the universe where Munter and Van used to be and to get Draska out of the house. But when Draska picks a fight with Kasey, Munter ends up smacking Van, again. Cheryl's plans to bounce Draska fail; in the end they strike a deal. Cheryl will tolerate Draska and Draska will look after Van. Meanwhile, when Loretta discovers that Hayden lied about alterations to her film and refuses to recall the DVDs, she declares their relationship over. Pascalle offers useful advice but Loretta has her own twisted plan involving revenge and a lot of glue. She is sure that this game will bring him back, then discovers that Hayden is leaving the country to escape her. She does what she has to: torches his place. Then, and only then, does she admit to Pascalle that she is completely and utterly heartbroken.

Episode 9 No Noble Rite
Pascalle is determined to be the best Muslim bride ever and to impress Bruce's sister Linda she insists on a hen party Is am style, with all the blokes banished to the pub. Linda however has decided that Pascalle isn't right for Bruce and invokes 'traditional' rituals — all to cause pain and suffering to Pascalle. Pascalle takes revenge in the form of a game of strip-pool but when the stripping goes too far, the girls are kicked out of the Rusty Nail by none other than Munter, who is now working behind the bar and, according to Grandpa and Judd, is taking the job way too seriously. Linda reveals why Pascalle is wrong for Bruce; she's way too good for her no-fun brother. Pascalle puts up a heartfelt defence and gets Linda's blessing. Pascalle is left to bond with Draska; they are the only ones who understand true love and marriage …

Episode 10 These Feats so Crimeful
When Pascalle sees how Van is taking advantage of Draska, she confronts him about his cruelty and how he has changed. Van breaks up with Draska, who takes this with dignity, knees him in the balls and is gone. Judd's court case is threatened when Hickey throws in a new complication; Sparky is missing and Judd is under suspicion of murder. Cheryl decides to find Sparky and she and Loretta go bush. Jethro is also feeling the pressure — fearing the cops might finally nail him for his part in the robbery. Seeing that Jethro is under threat, and knowing what this will mean to Cheryl, Judd makes a decision. He puts aside his pride and takes a deal. Judd is now a free man, though not exactly a rich one. And Sparky has come to stay.

Episode 11 Unpregnant of My Cause
Sparky's special senses alert the family to interesting news: Loretta is pregnant. It turns out she's four months pregnant and no way is Cheryl countenancing a late abortion; Loretta will be having this baby. Although Van seems to be healing, in truth he is contemplating suicide. Loretta has a horrible realisation about Van's state of mind and follows him to the forest where she makes an impassioned appeal. Loretta decides to have the baby if Van will promise to keep on living. They both resolve to go on, but return home to another disaster; Bruce has dumped Pascalle after seeing the porn film in a hotel abroad. Pascalle is distraught, but as Loretta points out, the real person to blame is Hayden. And by now, a three-man team arrives on the Gold Coast to deal to Hayden. But he is still taking no responsibility for the baby.

Episode 12 *Good Friends, as You are Friends*
Judd finally receives his police supercheque: 80 grand. Judd decides to pay his legal fees but finds that the bill has already been paid by Cheryl — with her loan from Gary. Judd approaches Gary who has a suggestion; Judd should buy into the business of a former cop and PI, Mike McCarthy. Meanwhile, Van, yet to make up with Munter, runs into odious Aaron 'ball tag' Spiller. Aaron's keen to be mates with Van, but Jethro is unimpressed, aware that Aaron runs a chopshop and is also a weasel. When Aaron's turf war with Falani turns bad, Van finds himself blackmailed into helping. But Van sticks up for Falani and Aaron turns on them as the cavalry arrive and Van is rescued by Jethro and — Munter. Cheryl and the family find that Van and Munter, at last, are back together.

Episode 13 *To Sleep; No More*
Cheryl and Judd are pushed into unknown undie territory when Kasey brings out the Love Sock and proposes it as a new Hoochie range. Cheryl is incredulous and Kasey accuses Cheryl of being a bossy cow. When Judd doesn't back Cheryl, her ire turns on him and the Love Sock war escalates between the Hoochie Mama partners and their partners. Van is mostly interested to know if Munter is wearing freaky undies, but is forced to don the Love Sock to settle the matter. Meanwhile, Loretta tries to assist Pascalle through all the stages of break-up post-Bruce. But Pascalle doesn't fall for Loretta's ruse and announces she's decided on a life of celibacy. The world has definitely gone weird.

Episode 14 *Natural Magic and Dire Property*
Various members of the West family find themselves in Gary's sights when Judd's security contract with Gary's company is cancelled and Jethro finds himself helping Gary's ex-wife Danielle. Van and Munter ponder their future careers and along the way discover that freaky things happen when they're separated. They need to find a career that will capitalise on the amazing united force that is Van and Munter. Cheryl goes to argue Judd's case with Gary, but is in for a surprise. Since Gary's been hit with a big bill by his ex-wife, he now claims he has no option but to call in Cheryl's loan. She has thirty days to repay the $120,000.

Episode 15 *Bow Stubborn Knees*
Loretta's big business plans are stepped on by an old foe, Irish dancing teacher Mrs Haggerty, but Loretta isn't going to let a jig stop her expansion scheme. Jethro steps in to assist Cheryl and takes on Gary, but gets short shrift, particularly as Gary suspects Jethro of helping Danielle. Facing further debts at Hoochie Mama thanks to Kasey and a container of leopard skin velour, Cheryl decides she'll have to visit Wolf in prison for his signature on a mortgage, only to find Wolf has been released. So where is he? With Grandpa stirring the pot about the spectre of Wolf, Judd is suspicious of where Cheryl has been. She reassures him with the partial truth that she was sorting out the fabric disaster. And she's come to a decision: if and when Wolf ever reappears, she wants a divorce.

Episode 16 *A Jig or a Tale of Bawdry*
Van and Munter proudly announce their new business venture: The Tool Guys — a 24-hour on-call handy service. Only Falani seems to take them seriously, but mostly so they can case houses for him. Given the ambiguous nature of their advertising, it's not surprising when a client wants extra service from the Tools. Van steps up and does the client while Munter does the guttering. To shield himself from temptation Munter proposes to Kasey, but she turns him down. Munter succumbs, but gets away with his indiscretion and Kasey accepts his proposal. And the Tool Guys decide on a Code, which includes no rooting of clients, not even blow jobs. Pascalle, meanwhile, gets jiggy with it and completes a jigsaw to find the meaning of life; which results in Judd and Grandpa bonding over work opportunities.

Episode 17 *The Secret Parts of Fortune*
Cheryl is desperate for money to pay her debt. After attending the wake of old colleague Lefty Munroe, Grandpa spots a photo that unlocks the past. Ngaire Munroe lets loose on Rita, leaving Cheryl and Loretta digging (unsuccessfully) for gold. Jethro's dodgy dealings finally work to everyone's advantage when he negotiates a settlement between Vern Gardiner, ex-commune leader, current City Councillor, and his ex-wives. Jethro then sells the land to Gary for a very reasonable price — but only if Cheryl's debt to Gary is cleared. Gary is keen to celebrate the deal with Jethro and they hit the town, but, when Jethro wakes up, everything has changed. He finds an angry Treena in his house making accusations of rape. What the hell happened here?

Episode 18 *Who Calls Me Villain?*
Jethro's many deals fall to pieces as he faces pressure from Cheryl, Gary, Vern and now Mr Doslic. On top of that, Treena's accusations of a brutal rape push him to the edge. Even though Van and Munter work out this is a ruse, Jethro finally faces up to the fact that Gary has outplayed him. But then he finds Cheryl has saved him by giving Gary half of Hoochie Mama. Meanwhile, Pascalle has a battle of her own at the Janet Frame when she defends Mr Purvis, a besotted inmate who has been filming her inspirational workout classes. But her rescue attempts are in vain, and Pascalle loses her job.

Episode 19 *Most Free and Bounteous*
Cheryl's new business partner, Gary, causes issues when he insists that his accountant takes over the Hoochie books. When he also suggests that they hold invisible parties for extra cash, Cheryl is faced with hurting her friends or standing by her principles. Van is suspicious of Gary's motives with Kasey, and with Munter out of town he's the only one who can save her honour. Cheryl decides to take the cash for the greater good, but at Kasey and Munter's engagement party all Judd can see is evidence of ill-gotten gains. As Munter makes his speech, Judd makes a decision and Loretta is left to tell Cheryl the bad news. Judd has moved out.

Episode 20 *Something is Rotten*
The Tool Guys are under pressure from Falani to pay their debt for secondhand tools, and from a client who won't pay. But when Falani robs the client to recoup his debt, the Tools find that crime doesn't pay too well. And Loretta, we find, has plans to adopt out her baby — preferably to rich, affluent types, for cash. She tries to scam the social worker, who turns the tables with blackmail — and demands a preferred couple of her own, the Colquhouns. Cheryl starts preparing for the baby's arrival, which appals Loretta, and she's finally forced to reveal her adoption plans. Cheryl is horrified, but Loretta's justification is that Cheryl has already changed the rules; anything goes and selfishness rules. Just like it always did. Cheryl is left to suck on that.

Episode 21 *The Corrupted Currents of this World*
Jethro and Van attempt an intervention with Cheryl, but this only angers her. They can sort the family if they're so concerned, and keep out of her life. So Van is left to sort out Pascalle (working at Nunga's bar and dating Aaron Spiller) and Loretta (pregnant and adopting baby out) but it's a hard ask, particularly when he also has to sort out Munter and Kasey's wedding. Van's job is made much harder when Munter is arrested for stealing Aaron Spiller's tow truck the night before the wedding. Jethro, meanwhile, is left to sort out the Gary problem and when all the dirt on Gary keeps leading to Wolf an unlikely posse of Jethro, Grandpa and Judd take a road trip to Whakatane to beard the Wolf in his new den.

Episode 22 *Where the Offence is, Let the Great Axe Fall*
Van's still on the job, keeping the news of Munter's arrest from Kasey on her big day. Judd, Jethro and Grandpa return from Whakatane, frustrated that Wolf gave them no dirt on Gary. Cheryl, via Gary, discovers Loretta's plans to sell the baby and imprisons her in her room. Pascalle saves the day by agreeing to appear at the wedding with Aaron, and in return Aaron will get Munter off the charges. Gary reveals that he's Rita's illegitimate son who wants back into the family. Pascalle's inspirational videos, meanwhile, have found fans via the web and an offer to work for the Sunset Channel in Florida. Wolf arrives with new bird Sheree in tow to sort Gary and attend the wedding. Van realises he's forgotten the rings. He races home to find Loretta has gone into labour; Van's first job as an uncle is to be a midwife. Wolf reveals all about Gary and Rita to Grandpa and Cheryl finds that Wolf is back, in cahoots with his stepbrother and with plans for the family. So where does that leave Cheryl?

SERIES 4
Episode 1 *Thinking Makes It So*
Pascalle arrives from Florida to find Cheryl has locked Loretta in her room and the cops and Plunket are swarming. But Pascalle's news is more shocking — she's married to Milt, the owner of the Sunset Channel! Wolf is unhappy with his princess's choice of husband but Pascalle has a new philosophy: Thinking Beautiful. Loretta, still planning on selling the baby, just needs to get out of her room, but Wolf and Cheryl unite and go to war with the Colquhouns. But it's Pascalle who solves the problem, as Beautiful Thinking manifests Corrina Balani and her latest unwanted baby, which is sold to the Colquhouns. So Loretta adopts her baby to Cheryl — on one condition — she gets to name her. So Baby Jane she becomes as Pascalle brings the family together for some reaching out and touching. But it won't be happily ever after. Loretta owes money to Wolf; who is suspicious of Milt; and Cheryl wants to finalise that divorce.

Episode 2 *The Edge of Husbandry*
Pascalle fears she could kill Milt with her body so, to everyone's shock, their relationship has not been consummated. Cheryl is horrified to find that Wolf wants to take half of the house *and* Hoochie Mama in the divorce settlement. Jethro's advice is to stay calm and wait for Wolf and Sheree to buy their own house — then Cheryl can go for half of Wolf's assets too. Van's melancholy is eventually diagnosed as loss of guy time with Munter. They join a blokes' night out as Wolf takes Milt to a strip club. Pascalle fears Wolf could kill Milt by putting his blood pressure through the roof, so Cheryl takes Wolf to task. But as she does so, she also reveals her divorce strategy. Milt stands up to Wolf and goes back to Pascalle, but as she's giving him her body, Milt drops dead.

Episode 3 As Much Containing
Grandpa sees Rita in a new light and Pascalle and Loretta struggle to counsel him. Cheryl blames the sudden appearance of a dodgy container outside Hoochie Mama on Wolf. When Sheree's brother, Nicky, arrives to collect the container, and it's disappeared, Cheryl suggests he check with Wolf. Actually, Jethro has moved the mystery container, leaving Van and Munter in charge. Van and Munter, unable to contain their curiosity, break in to find the container contains steroids. Believing they're helping Cheryl, they destroy them. Jethro gets his father to sign the property settlement in Cheryl's favour, then can't return the container. Wolf makes it clear that Jethro will have to leave town or face dire consequences from Nicky's associates. But Jethro knows his exile is also his father's revenge, because Jethro supported Cheryl.

Episode 4 Revenged Most Thoroughly
Grandpa looks for the Rita Rooter in old home movies, his plan: to find and kill the betrayer. Judd stops Grandpa, and finesses him into believing the culprit is already dead. But Loretta works out the real suspect is the kid next door who, it transpires, is none other than Vern Gardiner. Vern is surprised to meet Loretta, the spitting image of his first love Rita, and more surprised to find that Loretta would like to see him again. Wolf resents being Nicky's employee and hates the prospect of a mortgage, but arranges for Sheree to join the Hoochie team. Cheryl, angry with Wolf over Jethro's exile, takes revenge by ditching the invisible parties and going straight again.

Episode 5 Remorseless, Treacherous, Lecherous
Loretta has had a makeover that Pascalle and Cheryl find creepy and disturbing. Loretta uses her liaison with Vern to benefit her business. She further discovers that Vern might also be Wolf's father. The Tool Guys have a new job — working on Wolf's new house. Van's not keen, but Sheree is helpful. Wolf battles Loretta for money she owes him, but Loretta sees this as Wolf bullying his way into control of the family. She takes drastic action and approaches a drug-free Sparky for an arson job. The family is woken by Sparky's horror: the fire spread from the Video Hut to the pet shop next door and killed all the little animals. The family are aghast; Loretta is unrepentant. She stood up to Wolf that's all. But has she finally gone too far?

Episode 6 A Good Child and a True Gentleman
When Cheryl puts her back out and is laid up in bed, Wolf sees this as a golden opportunity to wrest control of his family as he visits Cheryl to 'help'. Sheree's not happy about this, but Van tries to cheer her up by fixing the plumbing. Wolf wins over Pascalle and chucks Loretta out of home, and when it is discovered that Baby Jane is missing, last seen with Sparky, Wolf and Judd compete to find her. Baby Jane is eventually brought home by Loretta, but there's no bonding moment here. And now the Tool Guys are wrongly blamed for plumbing disasters at Wolf's house. The real culprit is a vengeful Sheree, who has finally got Wolf's attention …

Episode 7 What is a Man?
Grandpa is disturbed that Wolf seems to be making a play for Cheryl. Sheree isn't happy either and as a result pashes Van. Munter points out that this is bad on two fronts: Sheree is Wolf's missus, and it's a breach of the Tool Guy Code. But the Tools have bigger issues when a builder called Rob, from Rob's Jobs, keeps stealing the Tool Guys' work. When Rob and sidekick turn out to be a chicks, Van and Munter fall out over the best method of dealing with the interlopers. Van finds that Munter is still bonking a client and Loretta uses the information to bring the Tools under her management. Grandpa, meanwhile, fears Judd is suffering from critical sperm build-up. He fixes him up with likely ladies, but in the end, Judd gets it back on with Cheryl.

Episode 8 Guilty Creatures
Cheryl is caught out when the IRD arrive to audit Hoochie Mama. Even though she's gone straight, the evidence of invisible parties is still in the accounts. The arrival of the IRD alarms the whole family, sending Van and Munter into hiding and Kasey into panic, but when Candice from the IRD needs custom-made undies, Kasey decides she's not so bad. Judd gives Cheryl unwanted advice that puts a dampener on their renewed relationship. Wolf discovers an unholy alliance between Nicky and Loretta and tries to keep them apart. Cheryl is surprised when the IRD is leaving without calling her to task, then finds Kasey has taken one for the team — only to be caught in flagrante by Munter. Her marriage is over!

Episode 9 Most Foul, Strange and Unnatural
The Kasey-Munter break up has its drawbacks for everyone, particularly Van, who is sharing a bed with Munter and doesn't enjoy the wake-up call. Loretta discloses that Munter is as bad, if not worse, than Kasey, and Cheryl evicts him from the house after he refuses to sort things with Kasey. Wolf uncovers Nicky and Loretta's secret — they're planning a robbery of Lloyd's bank. Nicky is keen to involve Wolf, but Wolf thinks the plan is flawed and forbids Loretta from getting involved. Wolf reveals to Cheryl that he's thinking of going straight, but first he must deal to his immediate problem — Loretta. On Cheryl's advice he speaks from the heart and Loretta seems moved by his plea. Then we find she still plans to go ahead with the job.

Episode 10 The King, the King's to Blame
The night of Kasey's birthday and a hell of a lot of stuff happens — including the big showdown between Cheryl and a jealous Sheree. From what we see first, it seems as if Wolf did the bank robbery after all and was caught red-handed. But as Cheryl confronts Wolf in prison about his claims that he wanted to go straight for her, Wolf replays what went down, and how he ended up getting arrested. He's realised that as well as wanting cash, Loretta's greater motive was to get Wolf. But she wasn't alone in the conspiracy; Wolf only went to stop the job after he was alerted by 'Van'. Wolf now realises this was none other than Jethro. (Who then rooted Sheree while pretending to be Van.) Cheryl confronts Loretta about what she's done and Loretta is unrepentant. Cheryl banishes Loretta from the family, along with Jethro.

Episode 11 Most Valiant
When Sheree proves to be useless as a crime wife, Cheryl intervenes to help Wolf, but Pascalle suspects deeper reasons. She confronts Cheryl about her feelings for Wolf, but Cheryl denies that she wants him back. Sheree is left on the street after Jethro sells his apartment, but Pascalle offers her refuge when Sheree turns out to be — pregnant. In this way, Cheryl is forced to put aside any feelings she might have had for Wolf. Meanwhile, Van and Munter find the car of their dreams and discover that Judd is sleeping with the law. And a new world order is established in the West: Cheryl has a house of women and Judd has a house of guys — including Aaron Spiller.

Episode 12 Let Them Throw Millions
To everyone's surprise, Milt's final bequest to Pascalle leaves her a multi-millionaire. Pascalle decides to distribute largesse, but her attempts to Do Good mostly result in annoying people. When Nicky dumps Loretta, she's sure he's after Pascalle's money and tries to warn Pascalle. Pascalle refuses to believe this, but Loretta is correct: Nicky and Sheree are hatching a plot to fleece Pascalle of her millions. But Loretta is on the outer with the entire family. Meanwhile, Van is confused by Sheree's insinuations about 'that night' — could he have sleep drunk-drove, auto-rooted her, knocked her up and not remembered? Van wants to confess to Wolf, but Sheree wants it kept quiet. However, she is prepared to jog Van's memory with a reprise root.

Episode 13 Your Chaste Treasure
Concerned he's losing his mojo, Grandpa agrees to steal a 'family heirloom' called the Duckeye of Rangoon for Ngaire Munroe. Loretta doesn't trust Ngaire and fears a double cross, then finds Grandpa has his own twisted motives — he wants to roger Ngaire. Grandpa gets the jewel and bests Ngaire at her own game. He doesn't get his root, but does regain his morning glory. Kasey is on with Dane Harris and Cheryl is appalled to find Dane has stolen Hoochie stock. Aaron Spiller steps up to defend Munter's honour and is rescued by Judd from a bad beating. Then Dane turns up after a beating and Kasey decides she can't leave him. Pascalle finds out it was Nicky who did Dane over, for Cheryl, and is impressed.

Episode 14 Rest Her Soul
Hayden's sister, Bernadette, forces Hayden home to face up to his responsibilities so Jane will get a Catholic baptism. Cheryl isn't keen until she finds Loretta is opposed. Jane is baptised, much to Loretta's chagrin, and Hayden bonds with Jane. Alone and rejected by all except Grandpa, Loretta sees that she's stuffed things up. Judd finds out Kasey has been buying pseudo-eph for Dane and is in peril, but Munter stubbornly refuses to step in. Fed up, Judd tells Munter to move out. Munter is goaded to action and tells Kasey to leave Dane because the cops are on to them. But when this doesn't stop Kasey leaving town, Aaron is determined to help and arrives to steal Dane's car. Munter appears, fights Dane and makes a heartfelt appeal to Kasey. They are reunited; Judd is a hero and Cheryl realises she's lost a good man.

Episode 15 Affection! Pooh!
Judd is wanted for questioning following a string of robberies at places protected by Judd Security. Judd is sure that Grandpa is responsible and Loretta knows his motive — he's trying to impress Ngaire Munroe to get into her knickers. Cheryl castigates Ngaire for her manipulative behaviour and believes Judd should throw Grandpa to the cops. Judd refuses and catches Grandpa in the act. Then Judd finds Cheryl has broken into his place to check he's okay. He sees that she does care, and it's all back on, at last. Elsewhere, with a little inspiration from Hayden and encouragement from Kasey, Pascalle comes up with an idea for a revolutionary new handbag. Sheree fears that Hayden is about to move on Pascalle and tells her brother to get busy. Nicky is helpful to Pascalle, then reveals his 'true' feelings. Pascalle cuts her ties to Hayden and Nicky is in. As Ngaire and Grandpa announce their engagement …

Episode 16 *A Sister Driven into Desperate Terms*
Alarmed that Grandpa is engaged to Ngaire and Pascalle is on with Nicky, Loretta tries to make things right. She warns Pascalle that Nicky's only after her money, and tells her about his part in the bank robbery, but Nicky talks Pascalle around. When Loretta walks in on Van and Sheree doing the wild thing she has ammunition for blackmail — but Van talks her around. Loretta apologises to Cheryl, who thinks the apology is owed to Wolf. When the Tool Guys are aggrieved with their huge workload, Loretta hires two new workers: Aaron Spiller and The Gooch, who turn out to be capable Tools. Threatened and unable to believe Loretta has good motives, Van and Munter fire the rival Tools, then rehire them when they find Loretta was sincere. As Loretta visits Wolf in prison to ask for his help …

Episode 17 *Dangerous Conjectures*
Cops find the remaining coin from the WSB robbery. Nicky accuses Loretta of taking his cash but she denies it — hers is gone too. Pascalle finds out Cheryl is pregnant, but Cheryl fears Judd's reaction. Meanwhile, Wolf is out. He tries to put Pascalle off Nicky, but beating him up only makes her more sympathetic. Cheryl finds out Loretta has helped Wolf get out of jail and begins to share her suspicions towards Nicky. Sheree coaches Van to hide their relationship from Wolf and announces she's pregnant with twins. But Wolf calls it quits with Sheree, only to have Cheryl tell him she's moved on. Annoyed that Cheryl hasn't told Judd about the pregnancy, Pascalle agrees to pay for Ngaire's dream wedding and also reveals Cheryl's news. When Cheryl does tell Judd, he's over the moon — as Wolf and Loretta realise they've been outplayed by the Greegans.

Episode 18 *Who Comes Here?*
It's Grandpa's wedding day and battlelines are drawn as the Wests take on the Greegans. Cheryl permits Loretta to attend the ceremony and also discovers Van and Sheree in bed. At the ceremony, a couple of wedding crashers arrive — Wolf with Jethro. Wolf warns Nicky not to touch Jethro and pav goes flying when Loretta and Pascalle come to blows. Van comes clean to Wolf about Sheree, but Wolf doesn't care. Later, when Jethro arrives home beaten up by Nicky and his associates, Pascalle's doubts resurface. Then Sheree reveals Nicky has been beaten up because of the Wests — but it's a ruse. The Greegans have set this up to finesse Pascalle out of her money. Wolf and Jethro are aghast to find Pascalle has given Nicky $100,000 to pay off the steroid debt and 'save' Jethro. Cheryl realises that Wolf orchestrated Jethro's return to get at Nicky, and rejects Wolf forever. Cheryl decides to take in Sheree to keep her enemies closer, as Pascalle asks Nicky to marry her. Cheryl is appalled at the engagement, so Pascalle walks out, leaving a family divided.

Quiz answers

1. Pat
2. 16th
3. Smith & Caughey's
4. On the freezer in her parents' dairy
5. Mrs Falani
6. A cuckoo clock
7. Bay
8. The Lucky Dollar Store
9. Jasmine
10. Caroline Darling
11. Prison guard
12. TK Samuels
13. Billy
14. Rochelle
15. Shadbolt High
16. *Jandal*
17. Jared Mason
18. Uncle Carlos
19. Monica Judd
20. A hunting trip
21. Treena
22. Dotterels
23. Isengard
24. *No Ordinary Thing* by Op Shop
25. The Horsemen
26. Steak knives
27. Barry Gibbs
28. The Phat Hard Crew
29. Old Googly
30. Five: prison guard, Hayden, Graeme, traffic engineer, Nicky
31. Chantelle Lazenby
32. Two
33. Jeanette, Mandy the Mauler
34. True
35. Corrina Balani
36. West Galleria
37. Herne Bay
38. Aurora
39. Tui
40. Whatever Happened to Baby Jane?
41. Bette Davis and Joan Crawford
42. Under a driveway in Kumeu
43. Nunga's
44. Muffy
45. *Prison Vixens*
46. Ted West, Bilkey, Phineas O'Driscoll, Lefty Munroe
47. Because he only had one testicle
48. The Duckeye of Rangoon
49. The Golden Accordion
50. Trapman Stierson
51. Tool = Van; Guys = Munter
52. Hamlet
53. Carmen J. Leonard
54. Tutaekuri Bay
55. The toilet
56. A party bus
57. *Blue Lady*
58. Bilbo
59. John Rowles Park
60. Four, she sold the fifth to the Colquhouns
61. Car doors
62. The Love Sock
63. Pakistan
64. Whakatane
65. Brandon
66. Anne-Marie Gibbs; she is Sparky's sister
67. Feeney Flooring
68. Greg Feeney
69. *OF* writer Tim Balme played Greg Feeney on *Shortland Street*. Last seen on the show, he was heading off to the Bay of Plenty to lay lino
70. Suzy Hong, Tracy Hong, Aurora, Sheree
71. Mrs Haggerty
72. Lionel Skeggins
73. Sparky
74. Yes
75. Suzy Cato
76. The Janet Frame
77. Mr Purvis
78. Hayley
79. Roxanne Wilson
80. She is married to Grant Bowler
81. Old Brown
82. Tui Kiwi
83. Her 'eggplant thing'
84. John Leigh, Jeffrey Thomas, Sara Wiseman, Ros Worthington, Greg Johnson
85. Robyn Malcolm, John Leigh
86. Chest freezers; he was trapped in one while playing hide and seek as a kid
87. Van
88. Eddy Bear
89. 14
90. Vern Gardiner
91. In a sleeping teepee
92. Graeme
93. Horse
94. Hemi Chrysler Valiant
95. Ahipara
96. Bernadette
97. Bronwyn Bradley
98. Dave Fane (Falani)
99. Kasey
100. Charlie and Pete

See page 51 for quiz.